Gay Conservatives
Group Consciousness and Assimilation

Gay Conservatives
Group Consciousness and Assimilation

Kenneth W. Cimino, PhD, MPA

Routledge
Taylor & Francis Group
New York   London

First published by

Harrington Park Press®, the trade division of The Haworth Press, Inc., 10 Alice Street, Binghamton, NY 13904-1580.

This edition published 2012 by Routledge

Routledge   Routledge
Taylor & Francis Group   Taylor & Francis Group
711 Third Avenue   2 Park Square, Milton Park
New York, NY 10017   Abingdon, Oxon OX14 4RN

PUBLISHER'S NOTE
The development, preparation, and publication of this work has been undertaken with great care. However, the publisher, employees, editors, and agents of The Haworth Press are not responsible for any errors contained herein or for consequences that may ensue from use of materials or information contained in this work. The Haworth Press is committed to the dissemination of ideas and information according to the highest standards of intellectual freedom and the free exchange of ideas. Statements made and opinions expressed in this publication do not necessarily reflect the views of the Publisher, Directors, management, or staff of The Haworth Press, Inc., or an endorsement by them.

Cover design by Karen M. Lowe.

Library of Congress Cataloging-in-Publication Data

Cimino, Kenneth W.
    Gay conservatives : group consciousness and assimilation / Kenneth W. Cimino.
       p. cm.
    Includes bibliographical references and index.
    ISBN-13: 978-1-56023-608-5 (case 13 : alk. paper)
    ISBN-10: 1-56023-608-6 (case 10 : alk. paper)
    ISBN-13: 978-1-56023-609-2 (soft 13 : alk. paper)
    ISBN-10: 1-56023-609-4 (soft 10 : alk. paper)
    1. Gay conservatives—United States. 2. Gays—United States—Political activity. I. Title.

    HQ76.85.C56 2007
    320.52086'640973—dc22
                                                                                          2006028221

This book is dedicated to the fifteen thousand gays and lesbians who lost their lives in the holocaust because they refused to "assimilate." Their deaths did not stop the original gay liberation movement, only delayed it. All of us owe a great deal to those who came before.

ABOUT THE AUTHOR

Kenneth W. Cimino, PhD, MPA, is a Visiting Assistant Professor of political science and policy at Drake University in Des Moines, Iowa. A former *Advocate* editorial intern, he has written numerous articles for advocate.com, the Gay Financial Network, INT Media, and CBS "Marketwatch," and has been a featured guest on radio shows such as "The John McMullen Show" on Sirius Out Q. Before entering the academic field, he worked for ten years in the investment banking industry.

CONTENTS

Acknowledgments

The only people with whom you should try to get even are those who have helped you.

John E. Southard

If I have seen further it is by standing on the shoulders of Giants.

Isaac Newton
Letter to Robert Hooke, February 5, 1675

While an acknowledgment section of a book often sounds like an Academy Award acceptance speech, the clichés that follow should not distract from the sincerity of the feelings of appreciation contained therein.

First, I would like to thank the scholars at Claremont Graduate University's School of Economics and Politics for their guidance, help, and interest. Special thanks are due to Annette Steinacker for her continued patience, statistical wisdom, and support. Thanks are also due to Henry Pachon for planting the seed of the need for a gay political behavior study. But most of all, I would like to especially thank Gary Segura for his assistance, encouragement, good humor, and pioneering spirit. He defines the word *friend* in every way. However, he illustrates the word *mentor* even more.

Next, as they say, a friendship is not a big thing, but it is a million little things. And I am lucky to have some of the best friends in the world. However, it is impossible to acknowledge all their support and contributions throughout my many years. Specifically, I would like to thank Bryan Hughes for his longtime support and friendship. He is

Gay Conservatives: Group Consciousness and Assimilation
© 2007 by The Haworth Press, Inc. All rights reserved.
doi:10.1300/5722_a

truly the best DJ in San Francisco. Also, I thank Eric and Hilary Tatum for their love and years of encouragement. I thank Sergio and Tuc for always giving me advice and a couch to crash on when I am in New York. I thank Frank Clark, Dave Kaplan, Dave Mohr, and Cassie Clemmons for everything each one has taught me. They have all been gifts in my life.

Third, I must thank my partner, Wayne. He has taught me that love is more than holding someone's hand, but it is looking outward toward a future, while still acknowledging the present. His support, kindness, humor, intelligence, and strength is unwavering and still surprises me on a daily basis. Even when he is away we are close in heart. Simply, he is my best friend.

Next, my grandmother, Connie, has taught me that a person is never poor when he has family. And I humbly thank God for the one he has given me. What I am about to write is a small acknowledgment to the many things they have given me. First, I thank my brother, Anthony, for teaching me to be headstrong in my beliefs—even if they differ from others'. Next, I thank my sister-in-law, Jamie, for the gift of acceptance, serenity, and tolerance. Next, I would like to thank all those immediate and not so immediate family members whose lives have touched mine. Last, I thank my parents, James and Sheila, for their kind words, generous spirit, faithful support, and, most of all, their unconditional love. Their love, perseverance, ambition, confidence, and wisdom has been a source of inspiration throughout my life. Truly, they live life by example.

Last, I thank everyone at The Haworth Press for making my dreams come true—especially my editor, Dr. De Cecco, for all of his wisdom and counsel. Finally, special thanks go to Todd Gunther for his many hours of editing expertise, book advice, and unwavering support.

Chapter 1

Who Are Conservative LGBTs?

Sexual orientation is an essential human quality. Individuals have the right to accept, acknowledge, and live in accordance with their sexual orientation, be they lesbian, gay, bisexual, transgender, or heterosexual. However, the U.S. legal system does not always guarantee the civil rights and protection of all people, regardless of sexual orientation. Prejudice and discrimination based on sexual orientation is still a fact of life in the United States, and until this changes, the need for lesbian, gay, bisexual, and transgender (LGBT) policy research is essential. Especially important is gaining an understanding of the political behavior of the LGBT community and its response to these prejudices.

Therefore, this book highlights why conservative LGBTs might join political groups that not only do not support policies that benefit the LGBTs, but also, in some cases, advocate prejudicial policies and make statements that are actively detrimental to the LGBT community. So why would any member of this group be willing to identify with and politically support candidates or a political party that adopts positions harmful not only to themselves but also their community? In fact, many liberal LGBTs believe conservative LGBTs are not only slowing down the LGBT political movement but also destroying the movement from the inside. Thus, liberal LGBTs fear that the greater the number of conservative LGBTs who support the Republican Party, the more likely the LGBT political movement will be less effective in creating positive acceptance of the entire LGBT community.

In a recent Kaiser Family Foundation (2002) survey, 66 percent of LGBTs identified as liberal, and only 7 percent stated they were conservative. However, the liberal LGBT views the gay conservative

Gay Conservatives: Group Consciousness and Assimilation
© 2007 by The Haworth Press, Inc. All rights reserved.
doi:10.1300/5722_01

as an oxymoron. For example, Richard Goldstein (2002) labels gay conservatives as "homocons" and detailed a conflict between the liberal "queer humanists" and the conservative "homocons": "The gay right exists, just as Jews for Jesus do, but it stands apart from the ethos that marks gays as a people" (p. 30). Also, the liberal gay intelligentsia are not taking the homocons' split from the LGBTs quietly. Goldstein, in both the *Village Voice* (2002) and the *Nation,* christens Bawer, Sullivan, Camille Paglia, and Norah Vincent as turncoats of the LGBT community. In addition, Larry Kramer, Michael Musto, and Michelangelo Signorile publicly "outed" Sullivan's dangerous online sexual behavior (aka Raw MuscleGlutes) to the media (in Goldstein 2002).

The gay political movement brought together by the crisis of AIDS has now broken the LGBT community into factions—each at the other's throat. The LGBT political fight is on between two extreme opposing groups. Recently, a *New York Times Magazine* article suggested that a conservative philosophy is increasing throughout the country especially on college campuses (Colapinto 2003, p. 1). Thus, the rise in gay conservatism may simply be part of this movement. Is the rise of conservative LGBTs another symptom of this phenomenon? Essentially, at the turn of the twenty-first century, the LGBT community is politically splintering apart a number of LGBT political organizers just trying to keep the gay movement alive at the national, state, and local levels. So, who are these assimilationists? How do homocons fit into the politics of the LGBT community? What are the political strategies used by assimilationists and the homocons to engage conservative LGBT individuals to participate in the political community? Thus, the overall question becomes, How does the conservative LGBT political identity fit into the larger picture of the LGBT community?

There are several examples in which conservative LGBT political activity conflicts with the general interests of the LGBT community. One of the most sensitive LGBT political issues is the constitutional rights of LGBT individuals to marry, which would grant them the same spousal rights as heterosexuals. A 2003 Massachusetts state Supreme Court case, *Goodridge et al. v. Department of Public Health,* ruled that LGBTs have the same right to civil marriages as their heterosexual counterparts. Many liberal LGBTs believe that they experience within their committed same-sex relationships the same joys and hardships as partners in heterosexual committed relationships, but they are denied the economic benefits that heterosexual married couples receive. According to the Human Rights Campaign (HRC): "There are more than one-thousand benefits, responsibilities and protections allowed under federal law on the basis of legal marital status" (Jacques 2003, p. 1). However, although heterosexual civil unions are recognized under the Constitution's "full faith and credit clause" between states, most of the nation's 49 other states have created laws to deny legal recognition of LGBT civil unions from other states and foreign countries.

Many conservatives (and, indirectly, conservative LGBTs) believe the "right to marry" is applicable to unions only between a male and a female. Stanley Kurtz (2003), a research fellow at the Hoover Institution, noted that gay marriage is likely to "take us down a slippery slope to legalized polygamy and 'polyamory.' . . . Marriage will be transformed into a variety of relationship contracts . . . in every conceivable combination of male and female" (p. 2). Kurtz (2003) cites Gabriel Rotello's *Sexual Ecology* (1997) on gay sexual behavior and its ideological barriers affecting monogamy between gay men. He added, "Married gay couples will begin to redefine the meaning of marriage for the culture as a whole, in part by removing monogamy as an essential component of marriage" (p. 4).

Currently, conservatives are arguing for a Federal Marriage Amendment to the Constitution that would allow individual states not to recognize LGBT marriages from other states. However, a constitutional amendment would also force states to prohibit LGBT marriages, even if the citizens created laws for the legal recognition of LGBT marriages. Thus, the question becomes, How can conservative LGBTs support an ideology and a party that threaten to create a "constitutional" amendment prohibiting civil unions and discriminating against them?

A few LGBTs, such as Andrew Sullivan (1989), have argued for several years that the LGBT community should have the right to marry:

> Gay marriage is not a radical step. It avoids the mess of domestic partnership; it is humane; it is conservative in the best sense of the word. It's also practical. Given the fact that we al-

ready allow legal gay relationships, what possible social goal is advanced by framing the law to encourage those relationships to be unfaithful, undeveloped, and insecure? (p. 20)

Also, it should be noted that Sullivan (2003) has argued that if George W. Bush's administration did develop a Federal Marriage Amendment, the GOP would lose the one million votes it received in the 2000 election as well as the support of Log Cabin Republicans for perhaps a generation.

Another divisive LGBT issue is whether LGBTs should be allowed to serve openly in the U.S. military. On November 17, 1993, Congress passed the National Defense Authorization Act, codifying in federal law, for the first time, a ban on military service by LGBT individuals, and by 1994, the Department of Defense began implementing the directive "Don't Ask, Don't Tell," which prohibits the government from asking service members about their sexual orientation but provides for subsequent discharge of anyone discovered to be an LGBT. The National Gay and Lesbian Task Force (NGLTF) reports that the "Servicemembers Legal Defense Network (SLDN) documented 968 incidents of anti-gay harassment from 1999 to 2000, up 142 percent from a record 400 violations the preceding year" (cited in Osburn 2000, p. 1). In fact, NGLTF cites that the "SLDN found that reports of asking and pursuing, which are prohibited by the 'Don't Ask, Don't Tell' policy, increased 30 percent in the same period" (cited in Osburn 2000, p. 1). Last, the NGLTF states that the "Pentagon's own review in March 2000 found pervasive harassment supported by an environment that encouraged anti-gay, lesbian, and bisexual treatment" (cited in Yang 1999, p. 12).

Many LGBTs believe individuals should be allowed to serve in the military openly and proudly and many disagree with the notion that having LGBT individuals in the military will destroy cohesion of military groups. For example, LGBT rights activist Frank Kameny, a veteran of World War II, noted that "to lower the quality of our armed services is to give aid and comfort to our enemies . . . giving aid and comfort to the enemy is a definition of Treason . . . anyone who . . . is involved in the exclusion of gays from our armed services is a traitor who should be indicted, prosecuted, tried, convicted, and hanged" (Kirchick 2003, p. 2).

Opponents to LGBTs serving openly in the military argue that by doing so such individuals would harm a military unit's ability to work effectively. In fact, Charles Moskos, Northwestern University military sociology professor (and principal author of "Don't Ask, Don't Tell"), believes LGBTs should be banned from the military because of "modesty rights for straights": "I should not be forced to shower with a woman. I should not be forced to shower with a gay [man]" (Varnell 2002, p. 2). In other words, military heterosexuals should not have to serve with LGBTs because they will be looked upon as sexual objects by the LGBTs and disrupt military cohesion.

Another issue dividing the LGBT community is centered on "hate violence" toward LGBT individuals. Hate crimes against LGBTs remain a controversial issue between liberal LGBTs and conservative LGBTs. Liberal LGBTs argue that the state and local governments should play a more significant role in dealing with hate crimes. They believe hate crime legislation will send a powerful message that the state and local governments will not permit crimes motivated by bigotry.

However, conservative LGBTs argue that state and local governments should not create legislation that specifically includes LGBT individuals. For example, Sullivan (1999b) argues that "the outcome of the Matthew Shepard case suggests that we do not need hate crimes laws" (p. 6). He follows up this statement by suggesting that the publicizing of Shepard's death by liberal LGBTs helps to "feminize" gay men and "has resulted in a damaging symbolic statement about who gay men still are in U.S. culture" (p. 6). He concludes that the number of LGBTs involved in hate crimes is nominal, and, thus, LGBTs need no special protection. If gays account for about 5 percent of the population, then "the chance of a gay American meeting the same fate as Matthew Shepard is about one in a million . . . or about the same as being hit by a railroad train" (Sullivan 1999, p. 6).

In summary, issues such as "gay marriage," the "Don't Ask, Don't Tell" policy, and "hate crimes" legislation demonstrate how conservative LGBTs and liberal LGBTs are at odds over fundamental LGBT civil rights. These examples show how conservative LGBT political activities conflict with general LGBT community interests. If the two groups continue to remain divided over these problems, prejudices and discrimination will continue to plague the LGBT community.

QUESTIONS

Specifically, I concentrate on examining conservative LGBTs in the community. Overall, I ask, How does one expect these elements to sway political identification or vote choices? In other words, why don't LGBT conservatives use sexual identity as the main group identification? Pamela Conover (1984) replies that "because group ties are more easily linked to politics, group interests may actually become even more relevant than self interests in the processes of political perception and evaluation" (p. 760). Thus, the individual homosexual might be more concerned about religious prejudices because homosexual groups often experience bias from religious groups. Therefore, at another level, LGBT conservatives may appear to focus on economics or other characteristics to determine political choices. For example, Do economic interests rate higher than race/ ethnicity interests? Thus, the central question becomes, Why are these issues more important for some LGBTs than for others?

Also, in examining minority political scholarship, I found some similarities. For example, Kinder and Winter (2001) discovered that African Americans believe racial solidarity is more important than social class, but Caucasians see it the other way around. Drawing a parallel it can be argued that sexual solidarity is more important for LGBTs than it is for heterosexuals.

TERMINOLOGY

Alfred Kinsey, Wardell Pomeroy, and Clyde Martin (1948) defined a homosexual as a person who engages in same-sex sexual behavior. The Kinsey Report is the published data of the sexual behavior of 5,300 Caucasian males, preponderantly from the northeastern United States (Kinsey, Pomeroy, and Martin 1948). Kinsey, Pomeroy, and Martin developed a 7-point scale ranging from 0 to 6. A 4, 5, or 6 on the "Kinsey" scale represented a homosexual male. Thus, an individual who identifies as heterosexual in terms of both identity and sexual behavior is represented by 0. On the other hand, an individual who identifies as homosexual in terms of both identity and sexual behavior equals a 6 on the scale. Interviewees were questioned and assigned ratings based on the Kinsey scale in nomenclature of both present and past sexual behavior. The Kinsey survey showed that "37% of the total male population has at least some overt homosexual experience to the point of orgasms between adolescence and old age" (Kinsey, Pomeroy, and Martin 1948, p. 623). Thus, Kinsey, Pomeroy, and Martin demonstrated that there is a larger frequency of homosexuality and homosexual occurrences than was first thought to exist.

In this study, the term *gay* is synonymous with "homosexual male" as defined by Kinsey, Pomeroy, and Martin (1948). Also, the term *lesbian* is used to describe the "homosexual female." The term *lesbian, gay, bisexual, and transgender community* designates the society of homosexuals. Kinsey, Pomeroy, and Martin explain that this is the aggregate of social relationships that may or may not partake in comparable well-being, but which do share strong same-sex identification.

ARGUMENT

Focus

Specifically, this research investigates the utility of group consciousness as an explanatory construct for the understanding of political behavior among conservative LGBTs. Group consciousness, as developed from the work of Miller (1981), theorizes that group consciousness extends political participation among subordinate social groups. However, much of the social scientific literature on group consciousness focuses on group identity and consciousness within the context of larger society. Therefore, a major part of the study will investigate "group consciousness" within the confines of the political behavior of conservative LGBTs. Overall, the study will develop and test hypotheses from group consciousness literature.

Second, the book relates to the particular group under investigation. The study argues that the employment of the theoretical perspective implied by ideas of group theory on the LGBT population will serve to emphasize conditions of LGBT political behavior that might have been missed in the past. The 2000 U.S. census shows that 5 percent of the population over the age of 18 sexually identified as homosexual, and in 1994 the National Opinion Research Center reported that in the top twelve central cities, 9 percent of men sexually identified as gay (Gates 2001).

Therefore, part of this research will develop knowledge of a large minority group that has been greatly ignored in past scholarship on politics in the United States. This is significant for three reasons:

1. The study of homosexuality has usually been approached from sociological, economical, historical, and psychological perspectives, but seldom political. Hence, the research lacks understanding of political behavior relationships in which LGBT groups function.
2. Although there has been recent political commentary on homosexual groups, such as ACT UP (AIDS Coalition to Unleash Power), there has not been specific research on LGBT conservatives. However, our understanding of the political behavior of the homosexual population is derived from generalizations about the LGBT community as a whole. Specifically, the research does not focus on conservative LGBTs.
3. While intersecting counterparts often occur, the magnitude of similarities can be determined only through empirical research and direct investigation of the conservative LGBT population living in the United States.

Hence, this book is engaged in three connected fields of inquiry:

1. The research will examine group consciousness and its relation to the political behavior of conservative LGBTs. Essentially, the thesis questions why LGBT conservatives identify with a particular group whose policies seldom benefit the individual LGBT.
2. The book investigates prominent characteristics of conservative LGBTs in our society. Basically, the research hopes to understand the political behavior of these individuals and to provide a composite of conservative LGBTs.
3. This book centers on the investigation of conservative LGBTs and does not focus much on questioning general stereotypes.

Hypotheses

The discussion of Truman's (1951) group theory suggests a number of general areas of concern that are explored in the following chapters. These include an examination of the circumstances under which individuals join groups. Specifically, this research investigates the utility of group theory as an explanatory construct for the understanding of political behavior among conservative gay males. Group theory, as developed from the works of Bentley (1908) and Truman (1951), theorizes that individuals join groups because they enjoy interacting with people who share similar interests and/or who are motivated by similar problems or disturbing events. Thus, these areas of concern were examined in reference to LGBTs, specifically conservative LGBTs, and the questions focused on shared interest characteristics.

Question Group 1

Why are some LGBTs conservative when the Conservative Party and the manifestation of that ideology in this society are so patently anti-gay and provide few if any policies, based on sexual identity, that benefit the LGBT community?

Do LGBTs disagree with the conservative term that is utilized by the neoconservative movement or the religious right?

In actuality, do LGBT conservatives politically view themselves as classic libertarians and not as LGBT conservatives?

Hypothesis 1a. LGBT conservatives generally define the term *conservative* in terms of limited government, thereby not perceiving any inherent conflict between being LGBT and being conservative.

Hypothesis 1b. LGBT conservatives believe conservative group policies do benefit them on economic, political, and social levels, but they do not see the need to receive policies in regard to sexual identity. In other words, it can be hypothesized that some other identity rather than sexual is more important in terms of policy formation for conservative LGBTs.

Hypothesis 1c. When choosing from a menu of personal identities, self-identified gay conservatives are more likely to select other personal characteristics, including income, ethnicity, social class, gender, values, religious beliefs, or others, as the most salient.

Hypothesis 1d. When choosing from a menu of personal identities, self-identified gay liberals are more likely to identify their sexuality as their more politically salient personal characteristic, rather than income, ethnicity, social class, gender, values, religious beliefs, or others.

Hypothesis 1e. Conservative LGBTs are more likely than liberal LGBTs not to view LGBTs as an oppressed group.

Hypothesis 1f. Conservative LGBTs *do not* feel there is an inherent conflict in being gay and being conservative, yet liberal LGBTs *do* feel there is an inherent conflict in being gay and being conservative.

Question Group 2

Specifically, this book is centered on conservative gay males in the LGBT community.

What are the individual levels that correlate personal characteristics, such as education and religion, with their political identification as gay male conservatives? Do demographics alone explain gay political behavior? Overall, how does one expect these factors to influence political identification or vote choices? In other words, why do gay conservatives not use sexual identity as the main group identification? Gay conservatives appear to focus on economic or other characteristics to determine political choices. For example, do economic interests trump race/ethnicity interests? Thus, the central question becomes, Why are these issues more important for some LGBTs than for others?

Hypothesis 2a. White LGBTs are more likely to be LGBT conservatives than nonwhite LGBTs.

Hypothesis 2b. Male LGBTs are more likely to be LGBT conservatives than female LGBTs.

Hypothesis 2c. Older LGBTs are more likely to be LGBT conservatives than younger LGBTs.

Hypothesis 2d. LGBTs with higher levels of education are more likely to be LGBT conservatives than LGBTs with less education.

Hypothesis 2e. LGBTs who are employed full-time are more likely to be more conservative than LGBTs employed part-time.

Hypothesis 2f. LGBTs with higher household incomes are more likely to be conservative than LGBTs with lower household incomes.

Hypothesis 2g. LGBTs who self-identify as religious are more likely to be conservative than nonreligious LGBTs.

Hypothesis 2h. LGBTs who self-identify as in partnered relationships are more likely to be conservative than nonpartnered LGBTs.

Book Model

Specifically, this book will observe the political behavior of conservative LGBTs in relation to political classifications. Therefore, the study proposes grouping LGBT individuals into one of five hypothetical types of group identity responses based on political power and social construction:

1. The "recluse" group is composed of LGBTs whose conservative values keep them closeted. Usually, this group is quiet about its sexuality out of fear. Some members are public figures who believe that publicizing their homosexuality might ruin their careers. A good example of this group is closeted celebrities or political figures.
2. The "player" group is labeled as conservative and politically outspoken. This group blaringly identifies itself as republican but is less enthusiastic about its sexual identity policy needs. This group eschews traditional views to "fit in" with what they describe as the heterosexual norm; in other words, they are assimilationists. Good examples of this group are Log Cabin Republicans, Republican Unity Coalition members, and some HRC members.
3. The "apolitical" group has no political preferences—conservative or liberal. This group is indifferent toward its sexual identity policy needs.
4. The "advocate" group quietly identifies itself as liberal, also known as the "quiet Democrat." Thus, it also includes liberal gay males with considerable resources to influence policy. However, while they do not fear acknowledging their sexual identity policy needs, they do not place major emphasis on them either. Many believe the LGBT moralist might be part of this

group. Good illustrations of this group are some NGLTF members, Stonewall Democrats, and the other HRC members.

5. The "outsider" group has members who are extremely visible
but are radically out both politically and sexually in terms of
policy needs. Hence, this group feels it does not need to conform to traditional societal values, such as monogamy, because
general society does not approve of them anyway. Overall, this
group has a Marxist point of view and sees heterosexuals as the
oppressors and homosexuals as the oppressed. Thus, members
of this group see themselves as wanting to be free or separate
from heterosexuals. Specifically, they believe the only way to
effect political change is through protests and sometimes violence. Good examples of this group are other NGLTF members.
Some radical group illustrations are ACT UP and Queer Nation.

Primarily, this book will examine the second group—assimilationists.

Approach

Most of my research was based on online LGBT surveys conducted by Harris Interactive for the Gill Foundation. The refined
anonymity of the Internet and the added privacy presents safety
to self-identified LGBT participants. Thus, the online surveys are
more inviting and encompassing for LGBT individuals. Also, online
LGBT survey results appear similar to other survey methods. For
example, comparable surveys conducted by telephone using conven-
tional random digit dialing (RDD) techniques identified between 2
and 3 percent of individuals as LGBTs (Gill Foundation 2001). Overall, Harris Interactive consistently determines the LGBT segment at
roughly 6 percent of the U.S. population sample—and find that they
are notably similar in most key characteristics, including income,
education, employment, race, and ethnicity (Gill Foundation 2001).
However, they note that the sample appears to be younger and
more male in the total U.S. population. Finally, the online surveys
will most likely reflect the views of better-educated, higher-income
respondents because they have access to computers that the poorer
households might not (and possibly the groups most likely to be
conservative).

METHODOLOGY

Interviews (Surveys)

I used the Harris Interactive online survey as a primary supplier of data for research, but it was not the only source. I supplemented my survey research with face-to-face, e-mail, and telephone interviews of members of both conservative and liberal LGBT political groups, such as Log Cabin Republicans and Stonewall Democrats. I contacted local chapters of the Log Cabin Republicans and Stonewall Democrats in several cities and requested to speak to the presidents of the local chapters. I interviewed 15 Log Cabin Republicans and 15 Stonewall Democrats throughout the United States. Overall, the study posited that most conservative LGBTs believe the role of government should be limited. Hence, from these interviews, I found several variables to support my hypothesis.

Harris Interactive Online Survey

The Gill Foundation directed the project OutVote2000—public opinion research targeting LGBT voters. The Gill Foundation's (2001) report detailed the analysis from people who participated in every aspect of the project. Harris Interactive supervised a postelection online survey on behalf of the Gill Foundation and in collaboration with the Outvote 2000 to which 13,000 individuals responded. The goal of the research was to analyze the 2000 election cycle and gather information about how LGBT issues affect votes. The outcomes of the online survey were as follows: 85 percent of respondents identified as heterosexual and 15 percent identified as LGBT, other, or declined to answer (Gill Foundation 2001). Thus, from this original number, 1,146 self-identified as being a member of the LGBT community. Data were gathered from November 30 to December 5, 2000 in the hopes of understanding better the LGBT community's attitudes about voting, public policy, and their openness about their sexuality. Overall, 10 percent of the LGBTs self-identified with conservative political philosophies, and 16 percent of the LGBTs self-identified with the Republican Party (Gill Foundation 2001). The study researched the demographics of these particular two groups. The raw data of the Gill Foundation's OutVote2000 collected for the 2000 census were used as a benchmark. The data represented a truer picture of the LGBT community because the 2000 census identified only same-sex households as LGBT individuals. This research will therefore provide a better understanding of conservative LGBTs as compared to both the OutVote data and the 2000 census.

The Gill Foundation and Harris Interactive research offers an important snapshot and a distinctively harmonious profile of LGBT respondents that models the broader populations on several key demographics. However, this research does contain a few demographic variations. Specifically, the research tends to represent a disproportionately male population, with a significant portion between the ages of 18 and 34. Most likely, this is because younger men are more apt to be online and are thus more open to inquiring and discussing their sexual orientation. Although when Laumann et al. (1994) used random sampling of face-to-face interviews and questionnaires to investigate same-sex identity and behavior, they found 2.8 percent of males self-identified as gay, while only 1.4 percent of the female sample identified as lesbian. However, my initial investigations of self-identified conservatives show that 66 percent identify as male and 34 percent identify as female, and this corresponds exactly to the Harris survey results. On the other hand, my examination of the age groups shows only 26 percent arebetween the ages of 18 and 34, whereas the Harris survey results indicate 50 percent. Also, my investigations of LGBT self-identified republicans show that 76 percent is male and 24 percent is female, and only 21 percent say they are between the ages of 18 and 34. Thus, my research goes to show that LGBT self-identified conservatives and LGBT self-identified republicans are both older and more male than the general LGBT community. Hence, it is my belief that LGBT self-identified conservatives and LGBT self-identified republicans do not view sexual orientation as having any type of impact on their political philosophies.

PURPOSE

Importance of LGBT Political Behavior

At first glance the LGBT vote seems insignificant, but, as Hertzog (1996) stated, "In the 1992 presidential election, self-identified LGBT voters were as numerous as Latino voters, and outnumbered Asian voters two to one" (p. 2). If Hertzog is correct, then his "lavender vote" hypotheses will reach 4 to 5 percent of the total voting population within the next 20 years. It is possible that self-identified LGBT voters will empower potential voting blocs larger than those of other minority groups, except African Americans and Latinos. Also, the LGBT stereotype implies that the LGBT political community has a strong bias toward Liberal and Democratic Party candidates. Thus, my goal is to view how many LGBTs would identify themselves as conservative and republican, and whether and to what extent they differ in their demographics, attitudes, and group development compared with the rest of the LGBT community.

In the past, political science has paid little attention to the LGBT community, but as new generations find it easier to be "out of the closet," the LGBT self-identity percentage will greatly increase. Thus, the field of political science lets the discipline down by failing to research this particular group's political behavior. In fact, Hertzog (1996) concluded that in 1992 only 4 percent of the population self-identified as LGBT. However, by the 2000 census, 5 percent of the population self-identified as LGBT (Gates 2001). Hence, this subpopulation needs to be understood in greater detail. Is this a cohesive voting bloc that can be tapped for future candidates?

Also, this research is significant because it is one of the first studies of its kind. Currently, only a few studies exist on the composition of the LGBT population, making it difficult to know the true demographic picture of the LGBT community. Even fewer studies have been conducted on the conservative LGBT community, if any at all. It should be noted that Harris Interactive is one of the few major research organizations that samples and segments panelists who identify as LGBT.

Problems in Studying Conservative LGBT Groups

This book approaches the topic of homosexuality from the perspectives of political behavior and group theory. However, there are a number of dilemmas in analyzing the subpopulation of conservative LGBT members.

First, there appear to be no previous studies on conservatives in the LGBT community. Thus, there is no model around which to build questions, nor is there an archetype to explain how this subpopulation is different from other minority groups, such as African Americans, Latinos, or Jews. Therefore, my model will start with archetypes from minority political identification and build from there. However, there may be differences because sexual identity is different from racial or religious identity. Also, there is a possibility of comparing this work with other studies of homosexuality that focus on more historical, psychological, or sociological aspects of conservative LGBT demeanor.

Finally, gay historian John D'Emilio (1983) detailed the growth of the gay liberation movement. He suggests the gay political movement corresponds with three periods of "punctuated equilibrium" (see Baumgartner and Jones 1993) or crises in American history in the past 60 years: World War II, the civil rights movement, and AIDS. Thus, the participants in this study are more likely to equate sexual identity with political behavior than with participants in the past. Hence, although this book plans to speak from a political perspective, it is important to review D'Emilio's (1983) three critical periods of the gay liberation movement. However, it might be possible that a fourth period is beginning to develop in response to the third period. The recent assimilationists' attack on the radical emancipation, moralization, and separation activists might represent a new crisis or disturbance in the LGBT liberation movement. Could the increase in conservative LGBT self-identification be in response to this possible fourth crisis?

Chapter 2

Review of Group Consciousness Theory

The goal of this chapter is to base my conservative LGBT thesis in a "group consciousness" model of political mobilization. Before I proceed to the group consciousness model, however, I review the literature that leads up to this archetype.

I believe that the basis of my description of group consciousness lies in the collected literature of political science. Therefore I plan to build the group consciousness model from group theory literature based on pluralism and political behavior, as well as the theories of political scientist David Truman.

The social scientific literature on group theory (Bentley 1908; Schattschenider 1935; Truman 1951; Salisbury 1964; Olson 1965; Axelrod 1984; Hansen 1985; Etheridge 1987; Sabatier and Mc-Laughlin 1990; Chong 1991; Walker 1991; Sabatier 1992; Nownes and Neeley 1994; Lowery and Gray 1995; Segura and Gartner 1997) has focused on group theory within the larger society. In *The Process of Government,* Bentley (1908) introduces the idea of politics as a group activity where bargaining, especially logrolling, plays an important role. In *The Governmental Process* (1951), however, Truman revived and expanded Bentley's contributions. Bentley's and Truman's studies tend to get lumped into the "political behavior" subfield of political science theory, so before looking at the group consciousness literature, I will build off of "pluralism" research to place the model in the political behavior subfield.

Gay Conservatives: Group Consciousness and Assimilation
© 2007 by The Haworth Press, Inc. All rights reserved.
doi:10.1300/5722_02

PLURALISM

Pluralism was first used for political theory in the early twentieth century. Harold Laski (1919), who was a committed socialist, lectured at Harvard, Yale, and London's School of Economics in the 1920s. He is the author of several books, including *Authority in the Modern State* (1919), in which he noted, "The monistic state is a hierarchical structure in which power is . . . collected at a single centre" (p. 346). But the advocates of pluralism wanted something different. Political pluralism is, therefore, a theory that power is, or ought to be, dispersed rather than concentrated. Three notions proposed in the U.S. pluralist tradition are the following:

1. In the 1780s, Hamilton, Jay, and Madison's *Federalist Papers* argue that multiple factions competing in the larger arena of a republic would balance one another out, offsetting the harmful effects of factions that would be dominant in smaller democratic societies in which one faction could become more dominant than the others.
2. In the 1830s, De Tocqueville argues that in predemocratic times, liberty was preserved when the aristocracy exercised a countervailing power to the monarchy. In a democracy, however, liberty could be threatened by the "tyranny of the majority." In *Democracy in America* (2001), he suggests that the free association of minorities outside of the government was acting as a countervailing power and that the tendency to form associations reduced the expectation that the government would do everything. Around the same time, John C. Calhoun proposed in *A Disquisition on Government* (1853) the notion of concurrent majority. He agrees with Madison that the solution is to extend the republic, concluding that a government of the people that encompasses many different interests is best.
3. In the 1950s, Dahl (1956, p. 30) revisits the *Federalist Papers* and argues:

   The making of governmental decisions is not a majestic march of great majorities united upon certain matters of basic policy. It is the steady appeasement of relatively small groups . . . to an extent that would have pleased Madison enormously,

the numerical majority is incapable of undertaking any coor-
dinated action. It is the various components of the numerical
majority that have the means for action.

In *Preface to Democratic Theory,* Dahl (1956) discusses the advent
of what he labels "polyarchy," which has several characteristics of his
later pluralist critiques of democracy. He admits that we are close to
this state, though we do need to make some revisions of our existing
system. As an example, if a number of citizens attain an "educated
conscience," then there is no need for "extended spheres."

Pluralist theory states that people group along economic, religious,
ethnic or cultural lines. People with similar interests form interest
groups, such as in the case in the early 1990s when there was a controversy about the spotted owl in the Pacific Northwest. Two groups,
the logging industry and environmentalists, fought over the right to
cut down trees. How can a conflict between intense minorities such
as these be settled democratically? Ours is a government of people
operating through competing interest groups. The plural model favors
a decentralized and organizationally complex structure to provide both
groups with access to public officials.

It is important to clarify that both Bentley's and Truman's research
examines interest group behavior and not Madison's "majority of
factions." Therefore, we must acknowledge that interest groups and
Madison's factions are not the same. An interest group advocates a
certain point of view, whereas a faction aims to control government
because of that point of view. Madison in *The Federalist Papers #10*
is concerned with a "majority of faction." He argues that the danger
of pure democracy is that of the majority faction, and suggests that
the "extended sphere" is a medium that filters out passion and allows
reason to rule (p. 235). Citizens can pursue their own interests, but
these interests restrain one another.

In the early to mid-1900s, the pluralist tradition evolved into the
political behaviorist school of thought.

POLITICAL BEHAVIOR

The original political behaviorist school of thought developed out
of market research in the 1930s. Political behaviorists largely used

the sociological approach during the first half of the twentieth century in determining voter turnout, mostly because the only available
political science statistics were census demographics. Paul Lazarsfeld
led the pioneers of electoral sociology at Columbia University and
introduced the sociological model in *Voting*. Thus, Columbia researchers explained 1940s elections with this model by detailing a
voter's religion, socioeconomic status (education, income, and class),
and region. Their research indicated that older white, wealthy, and
educated individuals were the most likely to vote. Lazarsfeld suggested that there was a clear association between voter participation
and many social characteristics, and therefore social variables such
as age, education, race, religion, and income level can affect an individual's vote, with education seeming to have the greatest impact on
who did and did not vote.

Lazarsfeld also observed individual voting preferences in order to
determine the impact of stimuli such as the media's influence on voter
behavior. He believed that people were influenced by associations,
and he developed a sociological model of causality.

Although the sociological model identifies social cues such as those
that the previous researchers found, it was very limited in its weighing
of continuity and stability in the electorate. It therefore had limited
value in detailing electoral change, and in 1948 the Michigan school
developed a more sophisticated understanding of politics. This new
understanding emphasized three attitudes: (1) a person's attachment
to a party, (2) a person's orientation toward the issues, and (3) a person's
feelings toward candidates.

Campbell et al. (1980) initially introduced the psychological model
in their 1960s book, *The American Voter*. A person's identification
with a particular party became the heart of the model, as it in turn influences his or her opinion toward both the candidates and the issues.
The model focuses on psychological processes behind voting decisions.

First of all, the model emphasizes the existence and importance of
a long-term component in voting decisions—party identification.
Next, it consists of two central insights: as individuals identify with
religious or racial groups, so do they identify with political parties,
and much like this religious affiliation, party identification tends to be
very stable and thereby should be viewed as a long-term component in
voting. In addition, the model views party identification as well as

candidate evaluations and attitudes toward major issues as the most immediate attitudinal determinants of the vote.

Overall, Campbell et al. conclude that a funnel of causality shapes voting decisions.

It should be noted, however, that many political scientists believe that in the past 20 years, partisanship has declined dramatically in the United States. If a voter's political party no longer appeals to them, he or she are in turn much less likely to vote. This disagrees with the author's theory that party identification is a long-term factor affecting voting and issues and candidate selection are short-term factors.

GROUP THEORY: TRUMAN'S LEGACY

A subfield of the sociologist school of thought is interest group theory, the main scholar of which was David Truman. In the early 1950s, Truman began his generalization of interest groups with the Aristotelian assumption that humanity is social in nature and therefore, will "naturally" build a divergence of interest groups. He states that "man becomes characteristically human only in association with other men" (Truman 1951, p. 56). He outlines that interest groups are a collection of individuals who "on the basis of one or more shared attitudes, make certain claims upon society for the establishment, maintenance or enhancement of forms of behavior that are implied by shared attitudes" (p. 56). He also states that there are three factors to interest group formation: shared interests, clearly identifiable social grouping, and formal origination. It does, however, require some type of shock or disturbance to mobilize these factors.

Truman also posits that group development is often in response to some type of disturbances or crises. He suggests that groups have sprung from disturbances of the estimated patterns of behavior, but that these disturbances tend to show a wide variety. Furthermore, Truman theorizes that groups develop to counter other groups and thus the propagation of interest groups is boundless. In other words, each citizen is an inherent interest group member and is inclined to create a group in response to some type of crisis, disturbance, or formation of a differing group.

Truman continues by stating that group individuals will have overlapping affiliations that develop into a long-term equilibrium. This equilibrium is maintained because every group has a corresponding opposite group. Over time, members and leaders must cooperate with other groups for long-term success. He does concede, however, that overlapping memberships often cause groups to battle over members' primary interests. When conflict does occur, however, leaders work to alleviate the discord and quickly reestablish the group balance. In response to irresolvable conflict, new groups develop and promptly reestablish the equilibrium. Thus, by extending memberships, interest groups create a stabilizing force.

In addition, Truman states that groups provide access to democratic representation. He believes that groups are legitimate articulations of strongly held beliefs and welfare. He also says that groups are abstractions in the mechanism of democracy, explaining that if an individuals' interests are threatened then they mobilize into groups by automatically coupling with similar thinking people. Therefore, interest group development is both a democratic and representative process because those individuals who voice opinions will join a group in order to be heard. In other words, the many democratic groups in society mirror the divergence of interests in the republic. Truman puts forth that potential groups are also represented in his model. In fact, he suggests that the essence of potential group formation confirms that the group's well-being is always being contemplated. If individual interests were not being met, new groups would organize to meet those concerns. Organizations even exist to represent individuals who are not even aware of their membership, such as the Airline Passengers Association.

Finally, Truman attempts to provide a systematic explanation of the role of interest groups. He defends bargaining, compromising, logrolling (vote trading), and group alliances as important and necessary aspects of the governmental process. Groups are means of compensating for the complexity and diffusion of power and multiple lines of access in Congress. Thus, all behavior of an individual is a form of group behavior and participation can be accounted for only in terms of the groups to which one belongs.

In 1951, Truman's focus on interest groups was innovative and induced an overabundance of subsequent research. He was correct in identifying that people do form groups because of shared interests. Truman fails, however, to recognize that interest groups often develop with consequential qualifications. Hence, shared interests are important, but under certain conditions.

As an example Moe (1981) states that automatic group development, based on shared interest, occurs when members desire incentives and conclude they will be victorious. Similarily (1991) Chong says that individuals join groups if they believe they can achieve group goals and if leaders are willing to support the movement. Walker (1991) suggests that people join groups to strive for collective action goals, but high start-up costs necessitate patrons to absorb the costs. Finally, Etheridge (1987) says that "the group goal is clearly important for individual decision making, and it can be demonstrated that it leads to significant collective action" (p. 43). Overall, these scholars endorse the postulate of shared interests, but each has highlighted elements that Truman failed to recognize.

Truman's (1951) "disturbance theory" in *The Governmental Process* states that groups "have sprung from disruption of the established patterns of behavior, but these disturbances show wide variety." His concept that individuals mobilize as a response to disturbance still endures today.

Of course, groups also develop from situations unanticipated by Truman. Thus, the literature suggests that Truman is partially correct. For example, in *Political Economy of Group Membership* (1985), Hansen says that people join groups when endangered and are galvanized by possible political gains. He suggests that group incentives correlate with individual situations. Knownes and Neeley (1994) state that crises or disturbances cause an "entrepreneur" to respond with groups forming out of the entrepreneurial actions. Similarly, Walker (1991) suggests that groups develop during social change, but patrons are essential to shoulder the burdens of the groups. Finally, Gartner and Segura (1997) say that some people pay costs for membership in advance of any political activity. Thus, before people can organize and mobilize on behalf of a group, they must, at the very least, recognize themselves as being part of a group or subpopulation that shares interests. Also, group members should share this identity with one another. They state that there can be no collective action until there is at least an unspoken recognition by the group's members that they exist.

Although these scholars differentiate special circumstances for group formation, they acknowledge that similar interests and societal disturbances are significant in group development. An implication of their findings suggests that there are more LGBT conservatives than you can actually see.

Overall, Truman's (1951) *The Governmental Process* was the chief research on interest groups in the early 1950s. Several scholars have debated and adjusted his hypothesis, but two of his discoveries still hold today. First, collective needs and objectives unequivocally stimulate individuals to create interest groups. Second, disturbances do play some part in group development, but they are only one of many. He crucially misses the point that interest groups are self-regulating and lead to democratic representation. Therefore, he never acknowledges that people do not have equal opportunity to organize.

For example, if I am an unwed minority parent of three children living in an urban area, joining an interest group might not be my first priority. He disposes of class inequality too easily. Also, he gives overlapping memberships too much credit because most likely they will impede mobilization rather than encourage it. Several other scholars, such as Olson, Salisbury, Axelrod, Chong, Walker, and others, further expand on Truman's group theory.

Chong (1991) indicates that through the tactics utilized by social movements, groups can increase the probability of movement cohesion and group solidarity. His model suggests that material incentives have only a minor role in arousing public-spirited collective action, whereas solidarity and expressive benefits are the main motivations. A realistic likelihood of success provokes ebullience among the members. Therefore, introductory accomplishment is the best response for the passivity of a movement, although boycotts and nonviolent protests are also examples of collective action that can accomplish the preferred outcome by strengthening the movement's ends and means.

Both the "bandwagon effect" and the "contagion effect" are additional illustrations of how the movement advances in drafting new members and solidifying its core activists' convictions. Nonetheless, Chong suggests that momentum is necessary to conquer the thresh-

old for the movement to accomplish political and/or social transfor-
mation. Finally, Chong points out that unconditional cooperators are
necessary.

GROUP CONSCIOUSNESS

Political behaviorists, such as Verba and Nie (1972), Miller et al.
(1981), and Shingles (1981), state that among groups the force mobilizing them is group consciousness. In fact, Miller et al. (1981) identify
four parts to group consciousness:

1. They define group consciousness as "identification with a group
   and a political awareness or iridology regarding the group's
   relative position in society along with a commitment to collective action aimed at realizing group's interests."
2. They state "polar affects" are strong positive feeling for one's
   own group and strong negative feelings for a "reference" opposing group. The concept is measured with the placement of
   groups on a "feeling thermometer."
3. They describe "polar power" as recognizing dissatisfaction with
   the relative power of one's own group contrasted to that of the
   conflicting "reference group." Groups that feel oppressed obtained high scores on polar power.
4. They state that "system blame" is the understanding that the
   power structure, not individual behavior, is to blame one's own
   group and the reference group.

Both Gamson (1968) and Shingles (1981) add a fifth component that
they describe as political efficacy: one's belief that political participation makes a difference.

In terms of LGBT group behavior, Hertzog (1996) cites Cass (1984)
in saying that "public self-identification likely occurs only once one
has developed the psychological qualities constituting 'group consciousness'" (p. 11). Browning et al. (1990, 1997) observe that the
levels of political incorporation of racial groups in cities are based
upon four critical factors: cohesiveness of minority groups, swing
vote in electing a liberal coalition, use of electoral strategy rather than
protest, and unified leadership. Only when two minority groups form

electoral coalitions are beneficial polices for both groups formed. Hence, political mobilization of minority groups is significant in creating electoral coalitions.

As previously stated, the coming-out process is generally considered to be the stage of LGBT identity formation that causes many homosexuals the largest amount of emotional and social discord. But Cass's 1984 study details a relationship between the willingness of the LGBT individual to come out to those family, friends, and co-workers with unknown (or possibly negative) responses to what African Americans and feminists depict as group consciousness. Therefore, among political LGBTs, such as Log Cabin Republicans, is the coming-out process their group consciousness as Cass details or does this group have a second group consciousness later in life?

Because many LGBT individuals prefer to conceal their homosexual identity, remaining "in the closet" rather than coming out, it becomes difficult to determine when political group consciousness occurs. Also, those LGBT individuals who do choose to come out often disclose their sexual identity in distinct ways and to unique groups such as family, friends, coworkers, and the general public. Thus, the group consciousness of coming out does not have a set pattern to follow; it is different for each LGBT individual.

Interestingly, Cass's 1984 research reports that when LGBT children grow up, they are unaware that they are homosexual. In fact, they grow up believing they are heterosexual. For example, boys are told they will fall in love with girls and girls are told they will fall in love with boys, get married, and have children. However, this is not the same for African-Americans, who early on, realize they are different by skin color. As Hertzog (1996) points out,

> Once this consciousness of difference is established, black children grow up knowing that they are black and female children grow up knowing they are girls, with each over time learning the attitude and behavior expected of them by society in these roles. (p. 9)

Although LGBT children do become aware of sexual identity, it is usually under the belief they are heterosexual. The decision for LGBT individuals to disclose their sexual identity, and the point to which it is communicated, is dependent on a divergence of both internal and external factors.

Internal influences are impacted by the dimensions to which the LGBT individual experiences negative attitudes that society usually holds toward homosexuality. Over time, this has psychological consequences that influence the LGBT individual's self-esteem and self-perception.

External conditions are abundant and usually include the camouflaging of the LGBT's sexual identity at the workplace. For example, the LGBT individual might fear the possible negative consequences that would result from divulging he or she is gay. Also, in some cases, the individual remains "in the closet" because he or she are not confident enough to deal with the judgment and disapproval of the society. In fact, society tends, to view homosexuality as a "sin" or a "crime against nature" and considers it to be a "lifestyle choice" rather than a genetic sexual identity.

Again, this confuses the lines of acceptability and leaves many LGBT adolescents feeling confused and marginalized (Armesto and Weisman 2001). Therefore, it becomes crucial for LGBT individuals to receive nurturing from social networks. However, most LGBT youngsters encounter quite the opposite and endure rejection by their friends and family (D'Augelli et al. 1998). Thus, it is only when the LGBT finally acknowledges that he or she is attracted to the same sex that group consciousness begins.

Cross (1971) and Downing and Roush (1985) highlight that such strong "external events" are what rouse African Americans and feminists to develop an identity in their particular groups. Hence, if the LGBT never experiences coming out, it is doubtful that their group consciousness will develop the same as it does for African Americans and feminists.

THE HOMOSEXUAL IDENTITY STAGES

Cass's model proposes that LGBT individuals go through six non-age-specific stages:

1. In the *identity awareness* stage, the LGBT individual becomes conscious of being different from heterosexuals. The LGBT asks,

"Am I gay?" Thus, the individual begins to wonder whether homosexuality is pertinent to their self-identity. Cass says that denial and confusion are usually experienced in this stage.

2. In the *identity comparison* stage, the LGBT individual supposes that he or she might be homosexual but tries to ignore it by acting heterosexual. The person wonders, "Maybe homosexuality does pertain to me." Cass details that the individual will accept the possibility that she or he may be gay.

3. In the *identity tolerance* stage, the LGBT individual begins to realize that he or she is definitely homosexual. The LGBT realizes, "I am not the only LGBT out there." Thus, he or she embraces the probability of being homosexual and become aware of sexual, social, and emotional issues that go with being LGBT.

4. In the *identity acceptance* stage, the LGBT individual begins to explore their sexuality and seeks acceptance in the LGBT community. The individual acknowledges, "I will be okay." The LGBT accepts, rather than tolerates, the gay or lesbian self-image.

5. In the *identity pride* stage, the LGBT individual becomes an active member and starts participating in the LGBT community. The LGBT acknowledges "[I want] people to know who I am!" Usually, the individual gets deeply involved in LGBT culture.

6. Cass describes the final stage as *synthesis,* in which the LGBT individual fully accepts himself or herself (Dubé and Savin-Williams 1999). Cass states that the LGBT creates a holistic view of self. The individual defines himself or herself in a more whole construct, not just in terms of sexual orientation.

After testing her six-stage hypothesis, however, Cass finds support only for a four-stage process:

1. Cass describes the *identity confusion* stage. The LGBT individual thinks of himself or herself as heterosexual and soon realizes that his or her sexual identity is not something he or she is trained to be.

2. She explains the *identity tolerance* stage. LGBT begins to seek out other LGBTs to meet social, sexual, psychological, and emotional needs. However, the LGBT still pretends to be heterosexual and only enters the LGBT community when necessary.

3. She details the *identity acceptance* stage. If the LGBT individual encounters positive experiences in the LGBT community, the LGBT slowly begins to come out to friends and family. However, the LGBT will still remain closeted for the most part.

4. She describes the *identity pride and synthesis* stage. The LGBT individual is virtually out to everyone and shares a strong loyalty to the LGBT community. The LGBT individual begins to see heterosexual (primarily antigay) society as a difficulty and that being LGBT is no longer a problem. But over time, the LGBT softens to heterosexual society and no longer cares about their opinions.

Similarity, Troiden (1989) in "The Formation of Homosexual Identities" agrees with Cass's homosexual four-stage archetype. He, however, explains that the individual LGBT progress through four LGBT identity stages during the formation of homosexual identity in relation to time. He suggests that each of these LGBT identity stages is age-specific.

First, Troiden details the *sensitization* stage, which begins before the onset of puberty. In this stage the LGBT individual has homosexual feelings or experiences without understanding the implications for self-identity. Hence, the LGBT individual begins to feel unlike his or her peer group and may be exposed to marginalization and negative labeling. Unfortunately, this process usually creates a negative self-perception for the LGBT individual and hinders their LGBT identity formation. However, usually during adolescence, this unsteady and perplexed sense of identity leads the LGBT individual into the next stage.

Next, Troiden descirbes *identity confusion* as the second stage. At this point the LGBT individual not only recognizes but also realizes that his or her feelings, behaviors, and actions are classified as homosexual. Thus, the adolescent LGBT individual struggles with an intense conflict between his or her accepted identity that he or she had as a child and his or her new, socially adverse identity. Troiden feels the young LGBT individual experiences stress because he or she is conflicted over his or her new identity. Thus, the LGBT individual handles the anxiety in one of the following four ways:

1. The LGBT individual might totally deny his or her feelings.
2. The LGBT individual purposely evades situations that may require him or her to own up to his or her natural feelings.
3. The LGBT individual conceals his or her true identity by acting as a heterosexual.
4. The LGBT individual just embraces his or her LGBT conscience and sexual identity.

Unfortunately, the young LGBT individual has to deal with these inner conflicts as well as the usual physical, social, and psychological developments associated with adolescence. Therefore, the emotional hardship is exceptionally troublesome for many young LGBT individuals and often produces LGBTs who experience low self-esteem, depression, detachment, and thoughts of suicide.

Next, Troiden explains that *assumption,* the third stage, occurs in early adulthood and entails the LGBT individual becoming more socially involved with other members of the LGBT community. Also, the LGBT individual begins to master how to handle the negative labeling and social stigma associated with their LGBT identity. As in the second stage, the LGBT individual adopts several coping mechanisms to aid them throughout this development process:

1. Troiden explains that *capitualization* occurs when the LGBT individual surrenders to the negative notion of homosexuality, but still proceeds to recognize his or her participation in the LGBT community.
2. He states that *minstralization* transpires when the LGBT individual imitates a stereotypical LGBT identity and often exhibits exaggerated homosexual mannerisms and characteristics. A good example might be young LGBTs suddenly dressing up in drag and walking down the street.
3. He then says that *passing* happens when the LGBT individual conceals his or her homosexuality, except to a close circle of acquaintances.
4. He describes that *group alignment* takes place when the LGBT individual enthusiastically embraces the LGBT community and the LGBT lifestyle (Troiden 1989). Overall, the process of the LGBT coming out chiefly transpires within the LGBT

community, and possibly later within heterosexual society. The coming-out process is probably the most significant and confusing period in the formation of the LGBT identity. Therefore, LGBT individuals often endure intense emotional turbulence during this period of LGBT identity enlightenment, which contains the psychological, social, and cultural process of recognizing oneself as an LGBT individual and the deliberate or accidental revelation of their LGBT identity to others in society (Beaty 1999).

In the final step, Troiden explains that only once the LGBT individual prevails over the many dilemmas confronted during this stage can the LGBT individual progress forward to the last stage, which he describes as *commitment*. He details that in the commitment stage, the LGBT individual is able to synthesize their homosexuality into their overall LGBT identity. Hence, the LGBT individual accepts, embraces and adopts the homosexual lifestyle. In this stage, the LGBT individual no longer struggles with inner conflict or has a necessity to conceal their LGBT identity from their friends, family, co-workers and society in general.

Sullivan (1984) supports Troiden's hypotheses. He concludes, however, that during preadolescence, LGBT individuals distinguish themselves as being distinct from their peers, although not in terms of their homosexuality. Therefore, he states that LGBT individuals go through an introductory stage of ignoring same-sex feelings, followed by a period in which the homosexual vigorously masks their LGBT identity. Only when LGBT individuals inevitably appear emotionally and socially equipped, they start the coming-out process (Dubé and Savin-Williams 1999).

The LGBT political identity is a recent phenomenon in the last 50 years. Hence, as general society begins to embrace and accept the presence of sexual minorities in their daily lives, so too must political scientists understand the LGBT community as an inherent political force. However, recent studies suggest there is a great need to develop better policy skills with which to analyze, comprehend, and advocate the LGBT's individual political conflicts and indirectly, provide a better grasp of the social disorientation that sexual minorities sustain and tolerate throughout most of their lifetime.

Although the field of political science has a long way to go, it is beginning to change in its comprehension of the processes and stages of LGBT political identity formation and of how these processes differ from those experienced by heterosexuals.

GROUP CONSCIOUSNESS AND MINORITY IDENTITY

Group consciousness is a central thought on how minority groups have overcome exclusion, discrimination, and many other obstacles to participate in American politics. It is an individual's feeling of solidarity with a group that makes collective action and its influence on the political process possible. Thus, group consciousness is significant because it explains how minorities achieve political incorporation.

African Americans

Political scientists first began to examine group consciousness in comparing how African Americans and whites participate politically. For example, it was believed whites were more politically active because of socioeconomic conditions. However, it was discovered after controlling socioeconomicl factors that African Americans are actually more active in politics (Orum 1966; Verba and Nie 1972). One reason was that group consciousness made politics relevant to African Americans' lives and gave them a reason to participate.

Bobo et al. (1990) determined that group consciousness occurs for two reasons: African Americans' overcompensation for exclusion, and ethnic community approaches. They did not, however, see a clear relationship between group consciousness and political participation. Miller et al. (1981), on the other hand, found that group consciousness occurs among subordinate positions, mainly among the poor, African Americans, and women.

Olsen (1970) discovered that African Americans who expressed radical identification were more likely to participate than whites, when controlling for education and income, whereas Shingles (1981) concluded that group consciousness causes political efficacy and trust to become inversely related to each other.

Tate (1994) developed questions on group consciousness based on four areas: discontent with group status, perception of discrimina tion, support for collective strategies, and group political efficacy. For example, she asked, "Do African Americans as a group have too much influence, just about the right amount of influence, or too little influence (in American life and politics)?" Overall, Tate believed group consciousness is a secondary resource and that church membership was far more important.

New Minority Groups: Asians and Latinos

Recent studies have found that a reasonable percentage of Asians and Latinos support a pan-ethnic identity. There is, however, a bit of variation in the level of attachment to that identity across subgroups (Jones-Correa and Leal 1996; Lien et al. 2001). Hence, most Asians and Latinos prefer their specific racial identity, such as Korean or Mexican. In terms of Latinos, Shaw et al. (2000) concluded three points: (1) more Latinos claim to vote than actually do; (2) validated turnout rates for Latinos were lower than turnout rates reported by other investigators; and (3) Latino group mobilization had the greatest impact. Graves and Lee (2000) determined that ethnicity directly and indirectly shapes important voting considerations and hence plays a major role in shaping voting preference. Cain et al. (1989) found Latino immigrants and subsequent generations identify as Democrat, but Asian immigrants initially identify as Republican. Subsequent Latino and Asian generations have not, however, developed a specific party identification.

Most studies on the political consequences of group identity among minorities center on group identification either more or less than group consciousness. Group identification is an individual's awareness of belonging to a group and a psychological sense of devotion to that group, but group identification alone does not induce political action. Thus, studies that focus on only group identification may not demonstrate a correlation with political participation.

Group consciousness, however, merges group identification with the political awareness of the group's position in society. Thus, an individual's group consciousness becomes a remedy for correcting and improving the group's status in the community (Miller et al. 1981).

The fundamental presumption of group consciousness is that group solidarity will create greater political participation. Unfortunately, differing group ideologies can actually discourage individuals to participate in political activities. Hence, LGBT liberals express group consciousness in that they want to change the status quo, while LGBT conservatives do not articulate group consciousness because they do not want to change the group's position in society but wish merely to fit in. Therefore, I reason LGBT conservatives are not experiencing group consciousness per se, but responding to their group identity of gender, race and class. In fact, I believe they do not place an importance on sexual identity or sexual group consciousness at all.

In summary, the main point of Chapter 2 was to center my conservative LGBT proposition in a group consciousness paradigm of political mobilization. It is important to me that this book reviews the political science literature, which establishes the footing of the group consciousness model. Therefore, I have explored social science literature on LGBT group consciousness and the LGBT coming-out process. Both literature examinations allowed me to position the group consciousness model in relation to the political mobilization literature.

[Handwritten margin notes: "✗", "✗✗✗", "!"]

[Handwritten note at bottom: "So no critique of group theory. Just assuming cons are identifying with a different group | rigid hierarchy"]

Chapter 3

Evolution and Impact of the LGBT
Liberation Movement

The previous chapters have provided an introduction to the literature on "group theory" and its relation to the LGBT community. Also
introduced were some hypotheses and ideas regarding various other
areas of interest, which will be explored in Chapter 4. However, in
Chapter 3 I hope to provide a chronological background of the study
in question. Specifically, this chapter focuses on group movements in
the LGBT community over the last 50 years. One thing that I find to
be central in gaining an understanding of the recent conservative
LGBT movement is that we educate ourselves about the types of gay
liberation events of the past. Overall, the primary assertion of the current LGBT movement is that its members represent an oppressed cultural minority (Marotta 1981; Adam 1987). Hence, the assimilation
movement marks the first time members of the LGBT community are
no longer presenting themselves as an oppressed class. In fact, leaders of the conservative LGBT movement want to be seen as anything
but oppressed. Thus, they want members of the LGBT to find similarities, not differences, with other groups in the society. At the end of
Chapter 3 the study presents survey results gathered from 15 leading
conservative LGBTs and 15 foremost liberal LGBTs.

Chapter 3 provides an introduction to the development of the LGBT
liberation movement and identifies the more salient features of group
theory; however, the intent is not to present a detailed documentation
of specific LGBT group movements. Overall, the chapter aims to illus-
trate the evolution of the LGBT movement and its impact on current
conservative LGBT assimilationists. It also provides an outline of

Gay Conservatives: Group Consciousness and Assimilation
© 2007 by The Haworth Press, Inc. All rights reserved.
doi:10.1300/5722_03

LGBT history, showing how each LGBT group action is connected to the LGBT group political activity before and after. Finally, I conclude the chapter with interviews from ten well-known conservative LGBTs and their impression on the assimilation movement.

The previous chapters provided an introduction to the nature of research on group theory and introduced the research of leading scholars of LGBT political movements; I now present a brief introduction of three, possibly four, LGBT group identity movements that have occurred over the last 50 years. Again, the intent of this chapter is not to provide a detailed examination of the gay liberation movement, but to highlight the evolution of LGBT group identity leading to the formation of the recent conservative LGBT phenomena known as "assimilation."

CREATING A GROUP IDENTITY:
WORLD WAR II—ORIGINS
OF THE GAY MOVEMENT

To begin our brief "History Lesson," John D'Emilio says that World War II was a defining moment for many gay Americans: "The unusual conditions of a mobilized society allowed homosexual desires to be expressed more easily in action. . . . World War II created something of a nationwide coming out experience" (1983, p. 24). Also, sex-segregated military services permitted homosexual men and women to develop gay identities that were often continued through their military discharges. In fact, D'Emilio tells that for many homosexual men and women their wartime practices became the basis upon which they developed a postwar life (p. 24). He theorizes that many gay individuals, once freed from their small town existences, decided never to return home and thus moved to large cities. These large urban areas allowed anonymous gay socializing and the development of a gay subculture (D'Emilio 1981, p. 31). As if it were synchronized, the 1948 Kinsey Report paved the way for the arrival of this new subculture. D'Emilio cites Kinsey's findings that "Persons with homosexual histories are to be found in every age group, in every social level, in every conceivable occupation, in cities and on farms, and in the most remote areas of the country" (p. 36). Thus,

D'Emilio details that during the 1940s, urban gay subculture "took shape."

By the early 1950s, Republicans, hoping to discredit the Truman administration, began making national security and the threat of communism major issues. Therefore, the persecution of groups engaged in "un-American activities" was set in motion. Soon, Kinsey's 1948 report was being misused to describe homosexual activity as extensive and destroying the country. D'Emilio says, "Senators culled information from the Kinsey study of the American male . . . that homosexuality was wide spread, that homosexuals came from all walks of life, and that they did not conform in appearance or mannerisms to the popular stereotype" (p. 42) and twisted it to support their own devices in the making. Homosexuals were forced to leave positions with the military, State Department, and the federal bureaucracy. The FBI maintained records on individuals thought to be gay and would visit them regularly trying to extract the names of gay acquaintances (p. 46). However, D'Emilio tells that these persecutions had a contradictory consequence. He states, "The attacks on gay men and women hastened the articulation of a homosexual identity . . . ironically, the effect to root out the homosexuals in American society made it easier for them to find one another" (p. 52). Underground homosexual groups developed to counter internalized and politically spawned negative attitudes, such as homosexuality as a sickness, or homosexuals being "less than." The early LGBT movement borrowed heavily from Marxist theory in that they represented an oppressed group dominated economically, politically, socially, and psychologically by what appeared to be a predominantly heterosexual society. Many of these groups, evolving from their ties to the Communist Party, soon sought political action on their own behalf.

The Mattachine Society

Five men founded the Mattachine Society in Los Angeles in 1951: Hay, Gernreich, Hull, Rowland, and Jennings. The group's name is based on the "mattachines": mattachines are mysterious medieval figures in masks believed to be homosexuals in the Middle Ages (D'Emilio 1983, p. 67). D'Emilio states that the goal of the grassroots organization was "to find ways to develop in its members a strong group consciousness free of the negative attitude gay men and women typically internalized" (p. 58). Initially, members surveyed the gay beaches in the Los Angeles area to study and validate the gay political climate and find out possible support for the setting up of a gay rights political organization. D'Emilio says the founders detailed, that "homosexuals remained largely unaware that they, in fact, constituted a social minority imprisoned in dominate culture" (p. 64). The Mattachine Society founders attracted members by hosting semi-public discussion groups and, in addition, by offering a cell-like configuration to shield members from exposure. Consequently, two more men (Gruber and Stevens) joined the original five and the Mattachine Society finally "took shape" (p. 67). In April 1951, the Mattachine Society founders composed a one-page document detailing the group's proposed goals: "the purpose . . . was to unify isolated homosexuals, educate homosexuals to see themselves as an oppressed minority, and to lead them in a struggle for their own emancipation" (p. 67). The group's first major political victory was in response to the arrest of original founder Jennings who was a victim of police entrapment in a Los Angeles park. The group created the ad hoc "Citizens Committee to Outlaw Entrapment" to generate publicity of the case. The group "advertised" the upcoming case by handing out leaflets in known gay areas after attempts to use the regular media failed. Jennings's case was thrown out of court after the jury deadlocked on the charges. The success of Jennings's case created a huge interest in the Mattachine Society, with the membership growing to 2,000 in the Southern California area by 1953. Another outcome of the Jennings's case was the realization that the media would not be supportive of gay issues. Therefore, a few of the Mattachine Society members launched a homosexual magazine, *One,* to cover gay subjects. Following on the heels of *One,* the Mattachine Foundation was created by the society's founders. D'Emilio says the founders believed a foundation "could also become the vehicle for conducting research as part of an educational campaign for the rights of homosexuals" (p. 73). He cites that, in a letter from Rowland to Hay, they had "set a movement in motion" (p. 74).

Nevertheless, Senator Joseph McCarthy's investigation into communist behavior in the United States in the early 1950s caused the Mattachine Society's leadership to change from its originally radical to more conservative perceptions. By the mid-1950s, most of the original group leaders left the organization due to their communist pasts. New leaders advocated group members to change their pattern of behavior to be seen as "normal" in society. Interestingly enough, they now asked Mattachine members to begin participating in research on homosexuality so as to allow professionals to act as their "agents of social change." D'Emilio states, "Accommodation to social norms replaced the affirmation of a distinctive gay identity, collective effort gave way to individual action, and confidence in the ability of gay men and lesbians to interpret their own experience yielded to the wisdom of experts" (p. 81). In summary, the original Mattachine Society leaders advocated militant action and promoted the idea that homosexuals were a minority group. However, the McCarthyism movement of the 1950s limited the organization's growth, and it quickly transformed itself into a more traditional association, literally battling with its *own* identity and goals. As D'Emilio points out, "The first round of conflict pitted 'radicals' against 'conservatives,' with the two camps standing on opposite sides of each question" (p. 91).

By the late 1950s, both the Mattachine Society and the Daughters of Bilitis (DOB), its lesbian counterpart, began telling members to "police" themselves if they wanted to achieve equality through group publications expressing the gay movement's point of view. However, in 1958, U.S. Supreme Court ruled that the postmasters must deliver *One,* which represented support for the discussion of homosexuality (lower courts supported the U.S. postmaster's claim that the magazine was indecent. D'Emilio tells, "Activists inferred that the ruling sanctioned the discussion of homosexuality, and in fact, homophile publications escaped any further legal action by postal authorities or local law enforcement agencies" (p. 115). Depressingly enough, by the early 1960s the gay movement had failed to mobilize constituents and little progress had been made with regard to changing social attitudes about gay public policy. To make matters worse, in 1961 charges by local Mattachine Society chapters that the national office had been misappropriating local dues, led to the ultimate disbanding of the national organization. Thus, after almost a decade of life, the gay movement seemed to fall apart. D'Emilio explains, "The movement took upon itself an impossible burden . . . appearing respectable to a society that defined homosexuality as beyond respectability" (p. 125). Ironically, in trying to accommodate social mores, DOB and Mattachine leaders themselves often reflected some of society's most condemnatory attitudes to their potential constituency. Their criticisms of the bars and gay subculture undoubtedly alienated many of the men and women with the strongest commitment to gay life. "If fear kept most homosexuals and lesbians away from the movement, contempt for its seeming acceptance of a negative view of the gay world may well have turned off the rest" (p. 125). However, by the mid-1960s, radical politics and the civil rights movement marked the dawn of a new era in the gay rights movement.

DELIVERY OF NEW RADICALISM:
THE STONEWALL REBELLION

Many believe that the birth of the gay liberation movement was on June 28, 1969, at the Stonewall Bar in New York. Barry Adams (1995) states that "drag queens exhausted of continual police harassment finally fought back and began to riot." Adams then goes on to say, "What made the Stonewall a symbol of a new era of gay politics was the reaction of the drag queens, dykes, street people, and bar boys who confronted the police first with jeers and high camp and then with a hail of coins, paving stones, and parking meters" (p. 5). Fortunately indeed, the new movement was not only centered in New York, but also throughout the United States. New gay militants grew out of the radical left movements, but focused on issues of gender and sexuality. Adams says, "Radicalized by their experiences in black and student organizations, they were now thinking through their own lives with new concepts and were taking a militant message to new constituencies" (p. 10).

Unlike the previous LGBT movements, gay political leaders used radical approaches the get their messages across. Soon gay liberation groups confronted police, picketed companies, and protested medical and psychiatric groups. Adams says, "The Stonewall rebellion in New York engendered a wave of new groups willing to take immediate, direct action against the old array of anti-homosexual organizations" (1995, p. 27). D'Emilio adds, "As pressure from gay liberationists made police harassment the exception, rather than the rule, in many

American cities, gay subculture flourished as never before" (1983, p. 231). One of the gay liberation movement's biggest successes was its assault on the American Psychiatric Association (APA) in the early 1970s, which resulted in the removal of homosexuality as a disease from the APA's official diagnostic manual, the DSM-IV. Adams states, "Leading movement activists reorganized as the National Gay and Lesbian Task Force to press forward the anti-psychiatric struggle" (1995, p 41). Though it resulted in the 1973 deletion of homosexuality from the APA manual, conservatives asked for a revote on the topic resulting in a 58 percent vote for deletion and 37 percent retention in 1974 (p. 49). Thus, the new manual allowed for a concession category in which psychiatrists could still treat people dissatisfied with their sexual orientation.

Ironically, by the late 1970s, capitalism quickly invaded the gender and sexually free utopian world, which the new militants had fought so hard for. Adams says, "The success of the movement in beating back stage management and repression of gay places allowed for a new generation of business oriented to a gay market" (1995, p. 49). One result of this movement was the creation of "gay ghettos" in cities such as San Francisco and New York. Another outcome was the development of a new masculine gay ideal—sexual, confident, materialistic, and nonrepentant. Adams adds, "As businessmen developed efficient sex delivery systems for gay men, a world of adhesive comrades and brothered a more remote ideal" (p. 101). The human relationship was replaced with a sexual one. Adams states, "Male bonding in the commercial gay world tended to impose into its sexual aspect, and those who did mange to make long-term commitments to each other often withdrew from the commercial world to do so" (p. 107). Thus, this new era marketed male sexuality to gay men; nonetheless, it supported the emotional distance gay men had experienced in their communities. Adams concludes, "The irony of the 70s, then, was the ease with which gay and lesbian aspirations were assimilated, contained, and overcome by the societies in which they originated" (p. 157). In a sense, gay men became trapped by a new male masculinity. In addition, lesbians were seduced by feminist nationalism.

Adams details that by the late 1970s, the conservative right re-emerged to combat the left. For example, State Senator John Briggs wanted to expel gays or lesbians and those who supported homosexuals from the California school system (Adams 1995, p. 189). San Francisco's Harvey Milk (finally elected to San Francisco's city council after several tries by appealing to the populist point of view) successfully debated Briggs on television consequently resulting in the failure of Briggs's proposition (p. 190). However, the gay and lesbian movement's celebration quickly turned to tragedy after former San Francisco supervisor Dan White assassinated Milk (and Mayor Moscone) a few weeks later. And within a year, San Francisco erupted in violence with gays fighting with police after White received the lightest possible penalty for the murders (he was out of jail in five years). Gays and lesbians were no longer going to let the police to push them around and began marching on city hall. Adams says, "This time gay people resisted, intended to seize their own destiny and conserve the small spaces they had so laboriously carved out of the cities" (p. 185). Finally, leaders of the gay and lesbian movement realized their sexual identity was the weapon they could use to fight the conservative right. In 1979, the Human Rights Campaign was started to raise money for pro-gay candidates and issues. Adams concludes, "Only by embracing it as an identity could homosexual desire be reorganized as collectivity capable of defending itself from its enemies" (p. 199). Sadly, an enemy from within would attack gays, in the form of AIDS. But the conservative right's failure to acknowledge the disease would soon reunite the gay and lesbian movement.

COMBATING AIDS: LGBT ACTIVISM

In the early 1980s, the "religious right" movement stimulated gays and lesbians to reunite and form a cohesive group. But it was the onset of the AIDS epidemic and the Reagan administration's inability to acknowledge the disease that caused the LGBT community to emerge, unified as never before. The "gay cancer" first appeared in highly populated LGBT cities throughout the United States, such as New York and San Francisco. Initially, it was the LGBT community that started noticing that their own were dying. In 1981, Larry Kramer said, "I must tell you that 120 gay men in the United States . . . most of them here in New York . . . are suffering from an often lethal form of cancer called Kaposi's sarcoma or from a virulent form of pneumonia that may be associated with it" (1994, p. 8). He concludes, "More than thirty have died" (p. 8). Conservatives were reluctant to have the government advertise ways to make gay sex and intravenous drug use safer because they feared it would be construed as an approval of deviant behavior. Also, low priority was given to the epidemic because it was not perceived as attacking the general population, but only high-risk groups (Shilts 1987). In fact, some religious conservatives, such as Jerry Falwell, suggested AIDS was God's "punishment on homosexuals" (Kramer 1994, p 6).

Kramer, in his frustration with the Reagan administration's lack of action to halt the spread of the disease, founded the New York Gay Men's Health Crisis in 1983 (Shilts 1987, Kramer 1994). He was later banished from the group as his aggressive style was damaging the group. Kramer not only attacked Reagan's administration, but also the LGBT community for its failure to be "self responsible," by doing things such as allowing bathhouses to operate. Kramer states, "I am sick of guys who moan that giving up careless sex until this blows over is worse than death" (1994, p. 46). His calls for radical tactics to get AIDS on the governmental agenda caused uproar in the LGBT community. By the mid-1980s, a number of national LGBT organizations began asking the government to make AIDS a priority. In 1985, the AIDS Action Council was formed to specifically lobby for AIDS. Soon after, the Gay and Lesbian Alliance Against Defamation (GLAAD) formed to improve the portrayal of the LGBT community. And with the death of Rock Hudson from AIDS in 1985, the disease finally became high profile. However, in 1986, the Supreme Court's 5 to 4 decision to uphold the right of states to criminalize "sodomy," as defined in Georgia as oral or anal sex by anyone heterosexual or homosexual, but not as a fundamental right for homosexuals. Therefore, the LGBT community has a long way to go.

Birth of ACT UP

By 1987, Larry Kramer and other LGBT AIDS activists frustrated with the lobbying groups' failure to make an impact with the Reagan administration, formed the AIDS Coalition to Unleash Power (ACT UP) in New York. ACT UP members used confrontation tactics, such as "die ins" at governmental agencies, pharmaceutical companies, churches, and on Wall Street (Kramer 1994, p. 13). ACT UP tried to force expedited testing and approval of AIDS treatment and to lower the high costs of AIDS treatments by drug companies (Crossen 1989; Kramer 1994; Signorile 1993). ACT UP was largely successful in getting both government and businesses to fast track AIDS treatment. Unfortunately, ACT UP was loosely structured and there was no national organization; therefore many chapters splintered or dissolved.

The Rise of Queer Nation and "Queerism"

ACT UP's initial success in getting AIDS on the government's agenda created an LGBT militancy by the late 1980s. One radical group known as Queer Nation organized to promote "queer visibility" (Signorile 1993). Queer Nation used slogans such as "We're here! We're Queer! Get used to it!" (p. 89), and conducted "Queer-ins" (same-sex kissing) in shopping malls (p. 89). Queer Nation, similar to ACT UP, believed the queer movement was signified by its rejection of the heterosexual mainstream. Thus, Queer Nation promoted shock messages to get straights used to it.

Queer Nation deliberately selected the word *queer* as an emblem of pride, just as the early LGBT movement transformed the pink triangle, the Nazi's symbol of homosexuals in concentration camps, as their own. "At the same time, the happy adoption of the insulting and abusive term for themselves would shock heterosexuals into paying attention" (Hertzog 1996, p. 11). Hence, the word *queer* represented all sexual outcasts, including transvestites and transsexuals. Thus, queer was meant to embrace and promote the acceptance of oddities and differences (Signorile 1993). In other words, queers were now "bashing back."

Outing

In 1989, Michelangelo Signorile, a former ACT UP activist (early media chair), and Gabriel Rotello, a New York party promoter, developed the New York LGBT magazine *OutWeek* in response to the media's failure to accurately cover AIDS and to "shake things up." Quickly, they began targeting the hypocritical media that allowed public figures to remain closeted. Signorile admonished, "You slimy, self-loathing hypocritical monsters, you go to your parties, you whirl with bigots and murderers, you lie and engage in cover ups, you sell your souls, meanwhile, we're dying" (1993, p. 68). Soon after the death of closeted millionaire Malcom Forbes, *OutWeek* outed his homosexuality, and a new controversy was born. Many in the LGBT community accused the *OutWeek* editors of practicing fascist tactics. Closeted executives in the media, entertainment, government, and business feared their reputations would be destroyed because they would be "outed" as gay. For example, in the early 1990s they outed gossip columnist Liz Smith because she publicized the "heterosexual" relationships of closeted actors and actresses. However, Signorile believed the only way for heterosexuals to truly accept homosexuals was to "breakdown the closet of power" (p. ix). In 1991, Andrew Sullivan wrote an anti-outing column in the *New Republic* after his friend Pentagon spokesman Pete Williams was outed. Thus, the backlash to the "in your face" confrontations began.

ASSIMILATIONISTS: THE BEGINNINGS OF THE CONSERVATIVE LGBT MOVEMENT

In the early 1990s, a small group of LGBT conservatives and libertarians began to rebel against "queer theory" and started to voice their opinions. They argued that LGBTs must begin to live in the "real world" and accept the dominant culture of heterosexuals. Hence, the "assimilationists" started a campaign to normalize homosexual behavior and present a better image to heterosexual society. The LGBT needed to get out of the "Disneyland" of the urban ghetto and try to assimilate. Thus, in their view, it was LGBTs similarities, not differences, with heterosexuals that are important. Two of the biggest names in the conservative LGBT movement are Bruce Bawer and Andrew Sullivan.

Bashing LGBT Radical Behavior

Bawer (1993) discusses homosexuality in a unique and traditional way. He complains that LGBT males are often depicted as promiscuous, effeminate individuals, often possessing few morals (p. 19). Thus, he not only attacks LGBT stereotypes, but also blames radical queers for causing the current misconceptions in our society. Overall,

Responsibilising gays

Bawer is disappointed with the LGBT community, and he criticizes them for the current problems. He feels that many gays are responsible for the misconceptions through their involvement in promiscuity and their flamboyant nature.

Bawer points out that he himself does not behave in this nature. He states that he is a conservative LGBT and is "normal" (1993, p. 25). He says he grew up in the society as any heterosexual did. Interestingly, Bawer describes himself as a model of decency. Hence, his book is an illustration of all that is wrong with the LGBT community and how certain things need to change. Bawer does not advocate that conservative LGBTs remain in the closet, although some might argue that his timid approach makes him appear as if he is in the closet. For example, he seems embarrassed about discussing his relationship with his partner, Chris. At times his relationship with Chris seems like an afterthought (p. 255); however, at the same time, he stresses that LGBTs need to set examples and stand up for what they feel is right (p. 246).

The heart of Bawer's argument is that LGBTs need to be accepted and fight against stereotypes. He attacks promiscuous LGBTs for their lack of morality. He is upset at that segment of the LGBT community that participates in "bathhouse" culture. It is his contention that it is this promiscuity that is damaging the image of the LGBT community as a whole. However, he points out that this type of behavior is also found in the heterosexual community.

Overall, Bawer's purpose for writing his book appears to be merely to educate the LGBT community in a new way. Simply, he is proving the ordinariness of the LGBT community. He explains that not only is the LGBT community not decidedly different from any other community, but also that it has the same responsibilities as any other community. In other words, the LGBT community needs to police itself on moral behavior.

Desperately Seeking Sullivan

Sullivan (1996) describes four political views on homosexuality: prohibitionist, liberationist, conservative, and liberal. His book "brackets the fundamental question of what homosexuality actually is" (p. 20). In his second chapter on "liberationists," he criticizes radical politics and details its relationship to Michel Foucault's social construction model. Sullivan says, "For the liberationists, the full end of human fruition is to be free of all social constructs, to be liberated from the condition of homosexuality into a fully chosen form of identity, which is a repository of individual acts of freedom" (p. 57). Particularly, Sullivan denounces the use of the word *queer* and its demeaning connotations.

Booker T. Washington, in his autobiography *Up from Slavery* (1901), makes an "essentialist" argument regarding African Americans and whites. Washington argued that making African Americans "whole" was so important that segregation was justifiable—if it helped in achieving this goal. Similarly, Sullivan and liberal LGBTs have the same "essentialist" debate. Washington reasons that it is the "essence" of African Americans, rather than their identity, that was the source of indignation to whites. Thus, he agrees with the idea that if African Americans conducted themselves in a manner consistent with white social expectations, all would be well. However, Washington knew this idea would be troublesome for the African-American community and could only be accomplished through education. Sullivan believes the problem with LGBTs is that the "drag queens," "butch dykes," and "leather aficionados" offend the "religious" folks. Thus, he reasons that if the LGBT community should try to fit in more, it would offend people less. However, Washington [*Sullivan*] went on to argue that the "essence" of homosexuals would still offend religious heterosexuals. Therefore, even if LGBTs wore suits and skirts, they would still not be accepted by the very definition of their being. Finally, as previously pointed out, in the 1950s, the LGBT community tried this before and hid their true identities, only to be sought out by conservatives.

Sullivan also denounces the practice of outing. He says this practice only makes the outed person feel ashamed. According to Sullivan, "Those outed are usually described as 'immoral,' betraying the cause of gay visibility, working in institutions which oppresses homosexuals, being insufficiently committed to the politics of gay liberation and the like" (1996, p. 79). Hence, it is his commentary regarding "queers" in this chapter that caused the LGBT community to become upset.

But Sullivan also criticizes conservatives. He does not understand how conservatives can hold LGBT to a certain moral standard and yet not give them the option of marriage. As I pointed out in Chapter 1, Sullivan argues that marriage should be a right for everyone. Also, he argues that LGBTs should be allowed to serve in the military— openly. He is totally against developing a constitutional amendment banning LGBT marriage; although he is strongly supportive of President Bush, who has expressed creating just such an amendment. Go figure! Finally, Sullivan does not believe that LGBTs need to be given special rights, such as hate crime protection.

Some liberal activists suggest that Sullivan's writings appear as being schizophrenic and inconsistent. For example, Sullivan is an early advocate for LGBT marriages as a way to lessen LGBT promiscuity. On the other hand, he now supports LGBT sexual freedom (although this change occurred after Sullivan was "outed" after having advertised for unsafe sex via the Internet). In the past, he has criticized LGBTs who participate in the hypersexual and drug-crazed frenzy of circuit parities. Yet, he details his attendance of, and indulgence in these very same circuit parties and their "freeing tribal effects," which has resulted in his appearing to be a conservative LGBT who is nonetheless still struggling with his own sexual identity.

GROUP IDENTIFICATION OF CONSERVATIVE LGBTs

As stated in Chapter 1, the study of the LGBT movement has most often been approached from a sociological or psychological perspective. Recently, Badgett and Rogers (1999) have examined the LGBT community from an economic viewpoint. Although Hertzog (1996) has explored LGBT voting behavior and Gartner and Segura (1997) have examined LGBT political representation, very few scholars have approached studying LGBT movements from an economic political stance. It is Hertzog's brief examination of group identification and its relation to the LGBT community that contributes to an understanding of LGBT group behavior.

Hertzog (1996) discusses Miller et al.'s observations on group identification (p. 9). Miller et al. (1981) say that group identification is "a perceived self-location within a particular social stratum, along with a psychological feeling of belonging to that particular stratum"

(p. 9). Therefore, group identification is the psychological conscious-ness of belonging to a distinct subset population. A sense that one's essential identity is bound up with that of other people who share some common attribute, characteristic, or belief (Hertzog 1996, p. 19). This corresponds to Truman's point that members join groups with shared attitudes; however, Truman also says that a group member "may not participate in those groups confined to persons of the opposite sex or of a differing age level" (p. 46). Therefore, one can reason that out LGBTs would not participate in heterosexual groups, but would so in only those groups that were of benefit to the LGBT community.

In certain occasions, group identification occurs among individuals with the "psychological desire to belong," but who have insufficient attributes that could provide them objective membership (Hertzog, 1996, p. 19). For example, Hertzog cites Bailey's 1992 study that dem-onstrates that members of the working class have a preference to identify themselves as middle class. Hertzog adds, "As individuals identify psychologically with the middle class rather than their own, their political attitudes and voting behavior comes to reflect those of their middle class far more than those of their working class neigh-bors who identify with their objective class" (p. 20). This implies that conservative LGBTs no longer—or never did—psychologically iden-tify with their objective sexual group identity. Therefore, conserva-tive LGBTs' group identification is with their class and social and/or economic identity. This is why conservative LGBTs rebel against Mattachine Society's doctrine of the "oppressed cultural minority" and do not believe they have been denied policy benefits. Also, the "assimilationists" most likely reacted to the crisis or disturbance they believed radical queer theorists were causing.

Chapter 3 has provided a brief review of LGBT group liberation movements. Also, this chapter focused on the evolution of radical queer theory to the current "assimilationists" movement and detailed some salient features of group identification. The main point of the chapter was to place conservative LGBTs and their movement within my theoretical model of group consciousness and political mobiliza-tion. In the following chapter, the study expands the definition of group consciousness as related to LGBT group identity. Specifically, I examine the group identity of 30 politically active LGBTs.

Chapter 4

LGBT Group Consciousness

This chapter draws together, and accounts for, some of the findings previously presented in light of available knowledge about the studies of conservative LGBT, in addition to my own study. The study examines a sample of 15 politically active conservative LGBTs (presidents of local Log Cabin chapters) and compared them with a sample of 15 politically active liberal LGBTs (presidents of local Stonewall Democrat chapters). The study primarily focused on the role of involved conservative LGBTs and their relationship to a group consciousness identity. Specifically, the data obtained support the general theoretical stance that one can find outlined in the literature on group theory and group consciousness. Thus, the intention of this study was to demonstrate that conservative LGBTs not only join together because of shared interests, but also that the conservative assimilation movement is a direct result of a disturbance or crisis in which conservative LGBTs felt threatened by radical queer theorists. At the end of Chapter 4, I present the study's interviews and detail several recognized differences between the two groups, in addition to a few similarities.

Campbell et al. state that neither one's political beliefs nor ideologies change much during one's lifetime. However, Jennings (1989) states that some individual adult experiences may impact their political behavior. But what about LGBT individual experiences in adolescence? Sherrill et al. (2003) explain that LGBT individuals rebuff their childhood "political socialization," preferring new political concerns as adults; although their research concentrates mainly on why so many LGBTs are democrats. They state that "as LGBTs become

Gay Conservatives: Group Consciousness and Assimilation
© 2007 by The Haworth Press, Inc. All rights reserved.
doi:10.1300/5722_04

aware of the differing stands of the two parties on issues of the rights of LGBTs, it becomes increasingly difficult for those who were born into republican homes to think of the Republican Party as good for 'people like us' " (p. 1). First, Sherrill et al. determined that liberalism is more an operation of self-identification rather than sexual identity. They point out that self-identified LGBTs are younger, educated, less affluent, and more urban—all characteristics of liberalism (Hertzog 1993; Sherrill 1996; Bailey 1999). Next, Sherrill et al. state that "being LGBT alters political beliefs and practices" (p. 1). Individuals who experience life-changing events, such as coming out, might reevaluate their party identification. Therefore, the stressful and shocking event of coming out serves to not only instil the individual's LGBT identity, but also to connect the LGBT individual to the LGBT community. Thus, the LGBT individual's group consciousness awakens. Finally, Miller et al. (1981) explain that group consciousness extends political participation among subordinate social groups.

So far the study shows that the LGBT's group consciousness begins with the coming-out process. Sherrill et al.'s (2003) research explains that, for the most part, LGBTs self-identify as liberal; however, they point out that LGBTs are more likely to question childhood political socialization due to politically socializing with a new group namely the LGBT community. Overall, they conclude that most LGBTs depart from their religious backgrounds and that active participation in their new LGBT community relates to ideology and partisanship.

DIFFICULTIES OF COMING OUT
(REJECTION OF GROUP CONSCIOUSNESS)

The LGBT individual's family remains the greatest factor in determining his or her decision to "come out" or not. Therefore, a person's family norms, values, and attitudes will most likely determine how supportive family members are to the positive well-being of the LGBT individual. Evidence suggests that parental rejection and family disappointment is a health risk factor for LGBT adolescents (Savin-Williams 1999). Some studies have shown that LGBTs who are rebuffed by their parents go on to encounter a multitude of emotional, psychological, social, and physical difficulties. Armesto (2001) states that LGBT coming-out problems range from Isolation to loneliness to suicide (p. 1). On the other hand, those LGBT individuals who have families that are accepting of their homosexuality tend to exhibit far fewer negative behaviors and report higher levels of self-esteem (Savin-Williams 1999).

There are also cases in which we find that some individuals, for a myriad of reasons, continue to deny their sexual identity until they are well into adulthood to the extent even going of through the heterosexual ceremonies of marriage and, sometimes, having children. Eventually when the LGBT decides to come out it is not one's family of origin that influences the LGBT individual's decision making, but rather, it would now be his or her relationship with his or her heterosexual partner and his or her children that takes center stage in the coming-out process for this individual. Many people in society are completely unaware of the enormous pressure exerted upon LGBTs with regard to divulging their true sexual identity in delicate relational situations such as these. Often the LGBT panics over the potential loss of his or her children in the courts should the marriage end in divorce, and if the LGBT parent were to be outed, what would be the of impact such a disclosure on his or her children. The LGBT's decision to live according to his or her sexual identity may or may not be pleasing to his or her marriage partner and/or supported by the courts in terms of divorce and custody battles; creating the possibility of a painful mess for all involved. In such situations, family counseling/therapy, with a counselor specializing in this particular area, would certainly be advisable prior to any major decisions being made regarding the couple and their children for the best possible solution for each of the family member. Doing so may well alleviate some of the hurt feelings and any misunderstanding; allowing the LGBT and his or her marriage partner to come to a healthy negotiating place before getting the courts involved. In addition, this further empowers each individual involved, including the children. Some researchers confirm that the feasibility of a child's potential rejection of a homosexual parent increases with age of the child. It would appear, then, that the younger the child at the time of disclosure, the better the prospect of that child embracing his or her parent as "being different" (Shernoff 1984).

As discussed earlier, the problems faced by LGBTs and their families are diverse and often continue throughout their lifetime, especially with regards to identity formation and the coming-out process. Unfortunately, depression, alcohol abuse, drug abuse, and suicide are but some of the potential side effects of real or perceived rejection faced by LGBTs as a result of "gay damage" attributed to the coming-out process. In addition, many LGBT individuals constantly struggle against widespread employment discrimination. In fact, some of the prejudice that exists toward LGBTs is commonly revealed in the form of dismissal from employment because of one's sexual orientation, as well as the verbal, mental, and physical violence an LGBT individual may experience just living day to day. It is certainly understandable, then, that many LGBTs never experience the true group consciousness of coming out. They would prefer to just "get along" and assimilate.

The next step in the study was to examine both conservative LGBT and liberal LGBT beliefs about gay conservatism and the "assimilation movement." In order to accomplish this, the study conducted interview with politically active LGBTs during the summer of 2003.

QUESTIONS

Why are some LGBTs conservatives, when the Republican Party and the manifestation of that ideology in this society are so patently antigay and provide little, if any, policies based on sexual identity that would benefit the LGBT community? For example, someone might point to President Bush's recent support of a constitutional amendment to ban LGBT marriages. Do LGBTs disagree with conservative terminology that is utilized by the neoconservative movement or the religious right? In actuality, do LGBT conservatives politically view themselves as classic libertarians and not as LGBT conservatives?

INTERVIEWS

Initially, I visited Washington, DC, to meet with the national president of the Log Cabin Republicans and the national president of the

Stonewall Democrats. Both presidents were informed that I would be contacting the local chapter presidents regarding participation in the study, which involved completing a 19-question survey on political gay identity and group consciousness. It is interesting to note that, although both presidents agreed to participate, neither returned the questionnaire. However, I was successful in contacting local chapter presidents through the national telephone contact lists of each organization, and the study participants were contacted via email and telephone. I told them that I would like to interview them for a dissertation at the Claremont Graduate School on gay political behavior. Participants were informed that completing the entire questionnaire would take around 30 minutes. Most participants returned the questionnaire via e-mail within a few days despite being given two weeks to do so. None of the participants asked to be interviewed over the phone and hence no interviews were conducted.

The study interviewed members of both conservative and liberal LGBT political groups, such as Log Cabin Republicans and Stonewall Democrats. Initially, 17 Log Cabin Republican local presidents returned survey questionnaires. However, when asked questions concerning group consciousness in an additional questionnaire, only 15 Log Cabin Republican local chapter presidents returned both questionnaires. On the other hand, 100 percent of the original 15 Stonewall Democrats local chapter presidents returned both questionnaires.

Although the number, of both conservative and liberal LGBTs interviewed was approximately 30, it is believed that a sample of this size is not sufficient to define the entire population of the LGBT community. It must also be noted that both samples were taken from politically active members in the LGBT community. Specifically, the participants were not only active in their local republican or democrat group chapter, but in most cases, were the president of their local chapter. The study found the sample population by contacting local chapters of both the Log Cabin Republicans and the Stonewall Democrats.

Participants were emailed a copy of the dissertation abstract (see Appendix), in addition to a consent form guaranteeing personal anonymity (see Appendix) accompanied by the questionnaire. The consent form stated that upon replying to the questionnaire via email, the participant agreed to be part of the study. All participants were informed that the interviews were confidential with each correspondence and each questionnaire sent via email reiterating the confidentiality of the participants. However, most participants appeared to be indifferent about the survey process and answering questions via e-mail. At the end of the my e-mail correspondence, the participants were informed that they would, upon request, receive a copy of the study once it had been published. Five participants expressed interest in this offer. Additionally, at the end of the interviews, the participants were asked whether there was anything the researcher had forgotten to ask. Only one participant added a new question.

THE INSTRUMENT

A two-page survey containing 19 questions was created. I purposely created a short one in order to help ensure response from the participants. The questions were developed from LGBT political movement literature. Most of the questions centered on understanding ideology and partisanship of both conservative and liberal LGBTs. The last ten questions were developed from Katherine Tate's African-American research (1994). Overall, the questions were geared toward comprehending LGBT political behavior and understanding group consciousness.

The following questions were asked:

1. What term do you use to describe yourself by sexual orientation?
2. What term do you use to describe yourself politically?
3. How do you generally define the term conservative? What does conservative mean in terms of government and its relation to the economy? What does conservative mean in relation to the society? What does conservative mean in relation to individuals and their private lives?
4. Do you see a need for the government to provide policies in terms of your sexual orientation identity?
5. Gays and lesbians are generally looking for greater acceptance in this and other societies. How do you think that should best come about? By heterosexuals being more accepting of gay and lesbian lives? By gays and lesbians better blending into the general community? Both?

6. What is your opinion of the gay political movement and gay activists? Are they too confrontational or not confrontational enough? Do you think gay and lesbian demands are too high, too low, or about right?
7. Do you see the LGBT community as an oppressed group?
8. What do you think most heterosexual Americans think of gay and lesbian people?
9. Do you feel there is any inherent conflict in being gay and being conservative?
10. Do you think what happens generally to LGBTs in this country will have something to do with what happens in your life? Will it affect you a lot, some, or not very much?
11. Do you think that the movement for LGBT rights has affected you personally?
12. People differ in whether they think about being LGBT—what they have in common with other LGBT members. What about you—do you think about this a lot, fairly often, once in a while, or hardly ever?
13. Which is more important, being: LGBT, both LGBT and American, or American?
14. Should LGBTs have anything to do with heterosexuals?
15. Do LGBT groups have too much influence, just about the right amount of influence, or too little influence (in American life and politics)?
16. If LGBTs do not do well in life, it is because: they are kept back because of their sexuality; or they do not work hard enough to get ahead?
17. To have power and improve their positions in the United States, LGBTs should be more active in LGBT political organizations; or each LGBT person should work hard to improve his or her own personal situation.
18. If enough LGBT vote, they can make a difference in who gets elected president. (Agree strongly, agree somewhat, disagree somewhat, disagree strongly?)
19. Please state how long you have been "out" to family, friends and co-workers. If not "out" to family, friends, and co-workers, please state "not out."

THEORY

Group Consciousness Questions

1. Sexual Orientation: The first question chosen for the study was the sexual orientation of the participants. Do they identify themselves as being gay, lesbian, bisexual, or transgender? The purpose of this question was to make sure the participants were indeed members of the LGBT community.
2. Political Philosophy: The next question of the study determined political philosophy. Thus, LGBT members who answered conservative or republican were placed in one sample; those LGBT members who answered liberal or democrat were placed in the other sample for comparison purposes.
3. Conservative Definition: The third question was based on the definition of conservatism. This question determined how politically active LGBTs describe the meaning of conservative, especially in terms of government, society, and individuals.
4. Role of Government: The next question was the role of government. How do politically active LGBTs see the role of government?
5. LGBT Acceptance: The fifth question was on societal acceptance of LGBTs. Do politically active LGBTs see a need to "blend in" or "stand out"? Or is it a combination of both?
6. Opinion of LGBT Political Movement: The next question focused on the LGBT political movement. Are LGBT activists too confrontational or not confrontational enough?
7. Oppressed Group: The seventh question centered on the oppression of LGBTs. Are LGBTs oppressed or not oppressed?
8. Heterosexual Opinion: The next question focused on heterosexual opinion of LGBTs. What do politically active LGBTs think of heterosexual opinions of LGBTs?
9. Inherent Conflict: The ninth question looked at the struggle of conservative LGBTs with a conservative political identity. Do politically active LGBTs see an inherent conflict in being a conservative LGBT member?

10-19. Questions 10 through 19 concentrated on the group consciousness of the study. These questions are based on Tate's
group consciousness study of African Americans (1993). Tate
developed questions on group consciousness based on four areas:
discontent with group status, perception of discrimination, support for collective strategies, and group political efficacy. Questions 10 through 13 centered on group status. Question 14 is
based on perceived discrimination in the LGBT community.
Questions 15 and 16 highlight LGBT collective strategies. Questions 17 and 18 observe political efficacy in the LGBT community. Finally, question 19 is structured to examine a link between
coming out and "group consciousness." The last nine questions
were created as close-ended questions in order to provide a sim-
ple analysis of group consciousness in the LGBT community.

PRESENTATION OF DATA

The following section is a brief summary of the data. More detailed data responses appear in Tables 4.1 to 4.27.

FINDINGS

Hypothesis 1a

LGBT conservatives generally define the term conservative in
terms of limited government, thereby not perceiving any inherent
conflict between being LGBT and being conservative.

Conservative LGBTs

Conservative LGBTs did not define themselves in terms of limited
government as much as I thought. Only 6 of the 15 participants, or 40
percent, defined themselves conservative in terms of limited government.

GAY CONSERVATIVES

TABLE 4.1. Overall data.

	Conservatives		Liberals	
	#	%	#	%
Conservative identity				
Limited government	6	40	3	20
Role of government	8	53	13	87
Acceptance—both	12	80	8	53
Too confrontational	9	60	2	14
Demands—just right	4	26	8	56
Not an oppressed group	10	67	4	27
Opinion—indifferent	5	33	4	27
No inherent conflict	14	93	6	40
Group consciousness				
Some impact	9	60	5	33
Affects personally	13	87	15	100
Think—once in while	8	53	3	20
American most important	10	67	0	0
Just right influence	12	80	6	40
Do not work hard	8	53	4	27
Should improve	8	53	3	20
Strongly makes a difference	8	53	9	60
Five to ten years out	7	47	2	13

TABLE 4.2. Sexual orientation: Democrats or liberals.

	#	%
Gay	14	93
Lesbian	1	7
Other	0	0

Note: Of the 15 participants, 14 answered gay or homosexual; 1 answered lesbian.

TABLE 4.3. Political philosophies: Democrats or liberals.

	#	%
Liberal	10	67
Democrat	2	13
Progressive	1	7
Moderate	2	13

Note: Out of the 15 participants, 10 answered liberal or liberal/democrat, 2 answered democrat, 1 answered progressive, and 2 answered moderate.

TABLE 4.4. Conservative definition: Democrats or liberals.

	#	%
Republican	6	40
Limited government	3	20
Averse to change	2	13
Traditional	2	13
Gave no definition	2	13

Note: Many people in society are completely unaware of the enormous pressure exerted upon LGBTs with regard to divulging their true sexual identity in delicate relational situations such as these. Conservative Definition—In defining the term conservative: 2 out of the 15 participants answered averse to change, 6 answered republican, 3 answered limited government, 2 answered religious or traditional, and, finally, 2 participants stated they did not want to give a definition.

TABLE 4.5. Conservative definition—Economics: Democrats or liberals.

	#	%
Fiscal responsibility	7	46
Lower taxes	4	27
Gave no definition	4	27

Note: In terms of economics, 7 of the 15 participants associated fiscal responsibility, 4 had an answer having to do with lower taxes, and, finally, 4 did not want to give a definition.

TABLE 4.6. Conservative definition—Society: Democrats or liberals.

	#	%
Pro-life	3	20
Traditional values	2	13
Exploit workers	1	7
Sacrifice programs	1	7
Restrict freedoms	1	7
Gave no definition	7	46

Note: In terms of society, 1 out the 15 participants answered conservatives sacrifice social programs, 1 answered that conservatives exploit workers, 2 answered traditional values, 1 answered conservatives restrict freedoms, and, finally, 1 answered conservatives are pro-life.

TABLE 4.7. Conservative definition—Individuals: Democrats or liberals.

	#	%
Interferes with life	10	67

Note: In terms of the individuals, 10 out of the 15 participants answered conservatives meddle in people's private lives, especially those of LGBTs.

TABLE 4.8. Role of government: Democrats or liberals.

	#	%
Yes	13	87
No	2	13

Note: Out of the 15 participants, 13 answered, yes, the government should provide policies in terms of sexual orientation identity, and 2 participants answered no.

TABLE 4.9. Acceptance: Democrats or liberals.

	#	%
Accept more	8	53
Both	5	33
Neither	1	7
Blend in	1	7

Note: In terms of LGBT acceptance, 8 of the 15 participants answered that heterosexuals should accept LGBTs more, 1 answered that LGBTs should blend in, 5 answered both, and 1 answered neither.

TABLE 4.10. Political movement: Democrats or liberals.

	#	%
Not confrontational	7	46
Too confrontational	2	14
Varies	1	7
Did not answer	5	33

Note: In terms of confrontation, 2 of the 15 participants answered gay activists are too confrontational, 7 participants answered that gay activists are not confrontational enough, 1 answered that it varies, and 5 did not answer the question.

TABLE 4.11. Political movement—Demands: Democrats or liberals.

	#	%
Too low	7	56
Just right	8	54

Note: In terms of demands, none of the 15 participants answered that LGBT demands are too high. Of the 15 participants, 7 answered that LGBT demands are too low, and 8 answered that LGBT demands are just right.

TABLE 4.12. Oppressed group: Democrats or liberals.

	#	%
Yes	11	73
No	4	27

Note: Of the 15 participants, 11 answered, yes, LGBTs are an oppressed group, and 4 answered that they are not an oppressed group.

TABLE 4.13. Heterosexual opinion: Democrats or liberals.

	#	%
Like LGBTs	4	27
Indifferent	4	27
Varies	4	27
Do not like LGBTs	3	19

Note: Of the 15 participants, 4 answered that, in general, heterosexuals like LGBTs, 4 answered that they do not think about it or are indifferent, and 3 answered that heterosexuals do not like LGBTs, and 4 answered that it varies.

TABLE 4.14. Inherent conflict: Democrats or liberals.

	#	%
Yes	9	60
No	6	40

Note: Of the 15 participants, 9 answered, yes, there is conflict between being an LGBT and being politically conservative, and 6 answered, no, there is not.

TABLE 4.15. Sexual orientation: Republicans or conservatives.

	#	%
Gay	15	100
Lesbian	0	0
Other	0	0

Note: One hundred percent of the participants answered gay or homosexual. And 1 out of the 15 participants answered that this was the first time in many years someone had actually come out and asked about his sexual orientation. He then said that people understood the participant to be homosexual because the participant was not married and because for those who knew about the participant's activism it was understood.

TABLE 4.16. Political philosophies: Republicans or conservatives.

	#	%
Republican	7	47
Conservative	2	13
Libertarian	1	7
Moderate	5	33

Note: Of the 15 participants, 7 answered that they politically identified as republican, 2 politically identified as conservative, 1 politically identified as libertarian, and 5 politically identified as moderate.

TABLE 4.17. Conservative definition: Republicans or conservatives.

	#	%
Republican	1	7
Limited government	6	40
Averse to change	2	13
Traditional	5	33
Gave no definition	1	7

Note: In defining the term conservative, 6 out of the 15 participants answered with a limited government answer, 5 answered traditional, 2 answered that they were averse to change (which could be interpreted as traditional), and 1 republican. Out of the 15 participants, 1 gave no answer.

TABLE 4.18. Conservative definition—Economics: Republicans or conservatives.

	#	%
Fiscal responsibility	5	33
Lower taxes	3	20
No regulations	1	7
Gave no definition	6	40

Note: Of the 15 participants, 5 associated fiscal responsibility, 6 gave no answer, 3 had an answer having to do with lower taxes, and 1 answered with a no government regulation response.

TABLE 4.19. Conservative definition—Society: Republicans or conservatives.

	#	%
More freedoms	5	33
Fewer regulations	5	33
Gave no definition	5	33

Note: Out of the 15 participants, 5 answered that conservative policies gave more freedoms, 5 answered with less government regulation responses, and 5 participants gave no answer.

TABLE 4.20. Conservative definition—Individuals: Republicans or conservatives.

	#	%
More freedoms	11	73
No answer	4	27

Note: Out of the 15 participants, 11 answered with provides greater freedom responses, and 4 gave no answer.

TABLE 4.21. Role of the government: Republicans or conservatives.

	#	%
Yes	8	53
No	6	40
No answer	1	7

Note: Of the 15 participants, 8 answered in the affirmative that the government should provide policies in terms of sexual orientation identity, 6 participants answered no, and only 1 gave no answer.

TABLE 4.22. Acceptance: Republicans or conservatives.

	#	%
Accept more	3	20
Both	12	80
Neither	0	0
Blend in	0	0

Note: Of the 15 participants, 3 answered that heterosexuals should accept LGBTs more, none of the 15 participants answered that LGBTs should blend in, and 12 participants answered both.

TABLE 4.23. Political movement: Republicans or conservatives.

	#	%
Not confrontational	2	14
Too confrontational	9	60
Varies	0	0
Did not answer	4	26

Note: Of the 15 participants, 9 answered gay activists are too confrontational, 2 answered gay activists are not confrontational enough, and 4 did not answer.

TABLE 4.24. Political movement—Demands: Republicans or conservatives.

	#	%
Just right	4	26
Did not answer	11	74

Note: Of the 15 participants, 4 believed gay and lesbian demands are about right and 11 did not answer.

TABLE 4.25. Oppressed group: Republicans or conservatives.

	#	%
Yes	5	33
No	10	67

Note: Of the 15 participants, 0 answered, no, they thought LGBTs are not an oppressed group, and 5 answered, yes, LGBTs are an oppressed group.

TABLE 4.26. Heterosexual opinion: Republicans or conservatives.

	#	%
Like LGBTs	3	20
Indifferent	5	33
Tolerant	4	27
Do not like LGBTs	3	20

Note: Of the 15 participants, 3 answered that, in general, heterosexuals like LGBTs, 5 answered that they do not think about it or are indifferent, and 3 answered that they do not like LGBTs. Of the 15 participants, 4 answered with tolerant, but not accepting.

TABLE 4.27. Inherent conflict: Republicans or conservatives.

	#	%
Yes	1	7
No	14	93

Note: Of the 15 participants, 1 answered, yes, there is conflict between being LGBT and being politically conservative. Of the 15 participants, 14 answered no.

The following are a few examples of limited government responses:

In a form unmolested by the undue influence of the Religious Right, "conservative" generally refers to that political approach which champions limited government, low and efficient taxation, support of the functional pillars of a free-market economy, individual liberty, and a strict constructionist's view of the Constitution. Business should not be un-

duly encumbered such that it is prevented from flourishing and producing jobs and wealth that invigorates the economy. Likewise, the
accumulation of wealth should not be punished nor stifled by a tax
code that seeks the deepest wells from which to increase revenue.
This punishes success and inhibits the very dynamic that represents a
vibrant economy in a free-market capitalist system. This is particularly
pernicious in light of the bloated and inefficient government spending
that progressives argue require a greater tax burden on those who
have accumulated some measure of wealth and self-sufficiency.

A conservative, in my judgment, is a person who seeks to conserve
the liberty and freedoms of the individual and contain the power of
government and its interference in the lives of citizens. From this philosophy, government should be limited, and its revenues curtailed so
as to limit its growth. Conservatives are also typically more willing to
hold the line on a doctrine of policy—domestic or foreign—and see it
through to the end no matter what the challenge, rather than change
course to cater to political pressure.

Less government and more free enterprise . . . the government's place
is not to regulate the personal or economic lives of its people.

A true conservative wants less government. This means less taxes.
Less interference in business. And keeping the government out of our
private lives and our bedrooms.

Liberal LGBTs

LGBT liberals also did *not* define conservatives in terms of limited
government. In fact, only 1 of the 15 participants, or 6 percent, defined conservative in terms of limited government.

Below is the illustration of the liberal limited government response:

A true conservative wants to limit the role of government in all aspects
of individual and public life. This has been distorted by more recent
conservatives who want to limit the role of government in all matters
except personal by their efforts to restrict personal freedoms.

Hypothesis 1b

LGBT conservatives believe conservative group policies do benefit them on economic, political, and social levels, but they do not see
the need to receive policies in regard to sexual identity.

Conservative LGBTs

I found that some conservative LGBTs *did* see the need to receive policies in regards to sexual identity, much more than I thought. For example, in question 4, 8 of the 15 participants, or 53 percent, answered that government should provide policies in regards to sexual identity.

A few examples of the perceived need for government to protect sexual identity responses are the following:

> The government's policies should mention sexual orientation only to the extent necessary to assure that sexual orientation is irrelevant— so that everyone, including heterosexuals, is treated equally under the law. Let's not forget that everyone has a sexual orientation, including heterosexuals.

> I need government to statutorily recognize that my rights as an individual are no different than those of any other citizen, despite others' attempts to marginalize or deny my rights on the basis of sexual orientation.

> Personally I would only seek to end public sector discrimination against LGBT people (arguable also is preventing discrimination by those doing business with the public sector). However, Log Cabin Republicans have taken a more interventionist approach to discrimination as does the most of the members my chapter.

> Yes, so government can remove discrimination, but so that it can initiate new policies.

> Only as it relates to overturning the policies that are targeted as discriminating in terms of sexual identity (i.e., laws that are on the books that target and separate sexual orientation).

> Only to sanction gay unions.

> Unfortunately, yes, even though some may say that does come into opposition with a conservative's basic beliefs in the role of government. I'm not sure that it really does. One of the founding principles of the nation is that individuals are judged on their individual merits, not on what their family name is, or what their title is, or how long they have held land in the area. We don't judge by the group. According to the Declaration of Independence, all men are created equal and are given by the Creator certain rights, among these, "Life, Liberty and the Pursuit of Happiness." I believe that it is wholly acceptable for the government to say that you cannot treat a person based on what he is; you must treat a person based on who he is. You have to judge him according to his merits in terms of his relationship to you. If it is employment,

it's his skills to do the job. If it's housing, it's in his ability to pay his bills, to keep the place neat and clean and to not keep the neighbors awake all night. It is permissible for the government to say to someone "You aren't allowed not to hire him because he's gay (black, Catholic, from the wrong side of the tracks, etc.). This is America. We don't do that." Part of the government's job is the protection of my right to earn a living based on my ability to do the job—on my merit as an individual.

Liberal LGBTs

However, a greater number of the LGBT liberals believed government should provide policies in regards to sexual identity. Moreover, 13 of the 15 participants, or 87 percent, replied with a yes. Therefore, I conclude that liberal LGBTs, more so than conservative LGBTs, want the government to develop policies that are based on sexual identity. In fact, the liberal LGBTs gave varied responses regarding social policies and sexual identity. Several illustrations of the liberal government policy responses follow:

> Yes, to protect me from powerful predators in the marketplace or in the legal structure who may want to force their old time religion on me.

> At this time, yes . . . since nonheterosexual identification is considered deviant and abhorrent to mainstream society in this country, governmental policies need to be implemented and enforced to maintain the rights, safety, and fair treatment of those who identify themselves as part of that minority.

> If by this you mean legislation for civil rights protection and basic equality where it currently does not exist—yes.

> Yes, in that we need laws that are blind to sexual orientation just as Martin Luther King promoted laws that were blind to color.

> I think government has the responsibility to pass antidiscrimination and antihate crime laws with respect to gay and lesbian, bisexual, and transgender Americans. I think government also should ensure that gay couples have the same property protections as nongay couples. I do not believe that the government has to sanction gay marriage, since my own view is that marriage is a straight institution that runs contrary to many of the values of the gay community.

> I need government—federal, state, all local—to provide just laws that are equally applied to all citizens. Whether I'm black, Jewish, one-legged, feeble-minded, or a conservative republican, I deserve the protections and rights of a citizen of this country.

> Yes, policies should be designed specifically for GLBT persons, rather than adopting the same policies straight people have.

Hypothesis 1c

Conservative LGBTs are more likely than liberal LGBTs to prefer members of the LGBT community to "blend in" with the heterosexual community.

Conservative LGBTs

I found that the conservative LGBTs did not want to solely "blend in" with heterosexuals. Thus, the conservative LGBTs were interested in keeping a separate homosexual identity from heterosexuals. However, 3 of the 15 participants or 20 percent believed that "heterosexuals should be more accepting of LGBTs." Therefore, a small number of conservative LGBTs felt the heterosexual community was not as welcoming as it should be. Notwithstanding, 12 of the 15 participants, or 80 percent, answered that the LGBT community should both "blend in" and "heterosexuals should be more accepting of LGBTs."

A few examples of "both" responses are as follows:

> Both. The groups simply need to get to know each other more.

> Both. General acceptance is a wonderful goal that may only be achieved by being "out" and by being yourself, maintaining your active role as a citizen and productive member of society. However, you can't force someone to accept you, and to try is a mistake. Acceptance will best come about when most or all gays and lesbians take the still bold step to live open, honest lives.

Sullivan-esque

> Gays and lesbians are not a "community" per se, and the concept that we all have the same values (outside of equal treatment under the law) or should live in the same places or share the same interests is a fallacy. It is also a fallacy to believe that we will ever be fully accepted in society, in the same way that bigotry and prejudice continues against others who have been marginalized in the past (Jews, blacks, unmarried mothers, etc.).

Bawer-esque

> Both. I believe it comes down to respecting others and by showing some courage. Not just courage in gay people not hiding but courage in the heterosexual world to question what they've always been told. Why should heterosexuals not accept gay people? How does accepting gay people harm them? If it doesn't, then is there a rational basis

for not accepting? I don't know how gay people can blend in any more than most of us already do. I have a few friends who I refer to as professionally gay, but most in their daily lives are largely indistinguishable from their heterosexual counterparts. They go to work in the morning, the grocery store on Sunday late afternoon, and fret about paying their taxes by April fifteenth. Flying a rainbow flag or having a sticker on your car is no more not blending in than is flying your alma mater's flag on game day. I'll admit that some gays do make asses of themselves in public, but they are many times guilty of the same sins they attribute to the heterosexuals they are trying to shock. They have already judged the heterosexuals as being nonaccepting bores who must be awoken and shown the error of their ways.

Critique of Queer action

Both, of course. All that separates the majority of heterosexuals being more accepting of gay and lesbian lives is education. Ignorance shields many intolerant views. Over time, with education (and the strides have been enormous in just the fifteen years since I have come out) things will get better. And part of the educating of America is the blending of gay and lesbian lives into the American community. It is all already happening before our eyes.

Liberal LGBTs

Also, I found that 0 percent of the liberal LGBTs believe they should "blend in" with heterosexuals; however, 10 of the 15 participants, or 67 percent, answered that "heterosexuals should be more accepting of LGBTs."

A few examples of "heterosexuals should be more accepting" responses are as follows:

Creating a new normal

As heterosexuals better recognize and accept the behaviors of gays and lesbians into mainstream society, those behaviors will be considered as less deviant and more "normal" thereby negating the need for gays and lesbians to work toward "blending in" better to mainstream society.

I think we need a spectrum of gay/lesbian expression just as we need that same sort of spectrum with any group. Naturally, in all groups everyone clusters toward the middle anyway (we already blend most of the time). The 10 percent fringe element of any group will garner 90 percent of the attention. This is okay. I think we just need to be OUT so we are visible. Silence truly does equal death, and visibility equals acceptance . . . over time.

I don't care for the blend in concept. I think the LGBT community needs to work on being more visible, not so much blending in, but standing out. We've been far too good at blending in the closet. It is critical for LGBT to be out so the stereotypes of LGBT are lessened and the reality is better represented. At the same time it's important for LGBT to not renounce or ignore it's more flamboyant and marvellous elements.

Time is on our side as education, and exposure, continues to make us just like them. Heterosexuals will become more accepting as more LGBT folks come out and they learn that their fathers, mothers, sisters, brothers, uncles and aunts, teachers, doctors, generals, etc., are gay or lesbian and they are no different. They will become more accepting through exposure in music, movies, TV, etc., to gays and lesbians. It is likely as the culture becomes more accepting and reaches the point of most folks just not caring what you are, then LGBT will just naturally blend in. In the meantime, we need to be out of the closet, we need to be pushy with our demand for equality, we need our parades and festivals to empower us.

I definitely believe heterosexuals need to be more accepting of gay and lesbian lives. Heterosexuals need to learn the definition of the word tolerance. Also, its time for white liberal heterosexual males (Clinton) to live up to their political promises.

We gain acceptance by just being ourselves everyday—indirectly impacting heterosexuals. We need to be true to ourselves and not hide our true self. We don't need to fit in, but truthfully exist.

Hypothesis 1d

Conservative LGBTs are more likely than liberal LGBTs to view gay activist's demands as too demanding.

Conservative LGBTs

I found that some conservative LGBTs are more likely than liberal LGBTs to view gay activist's demands as too demanding and gay activists are too confrontational. For example, in question 6, 9 of the 15 participants, or 60 percent, answered that LGBT demands are too high. A few examples of "too high" responses are as follows:

> There is no single gay political movement. But what is generally known as the liberal gay movement generally demands in too confrontational of a way. They can't really expect others to respond positively to that method. But if not for them, we moderate/conservative activists wouldn't seem so reasonable. The combination of the two is a workable balance.

At this time it's too high. I believe that a balance and broad approach is necessary to achieve our legislative goals. Confrontation is important, but only when balanced with those who argue rationally. Martin Luther King Jr. looked rational in contrast to Malcolm X and others who were radical or violent in their approach to demanding change—but he was still an activist.

Balance means that efforts must be made to influence ALL political parties, not just those we worked to educate 30 years ago and who will (today) TELL us anything we want to hear, but have not demonstrated with ACTION what we want to happen.

Politics is the art of getting something done. We need to educate and work with those in both major political parties (and the minor parties as well) to achieve our legislative goals.

If the goal is to be treated equally under the law, then our demands are not "too high." But, if we are demanding acceptance, then that will never be achieved legislatively.

For most of its life, the gay political establishment has been reactionary. One day years ago an left-wing elite got together and dictated what the "agenda" would be and has been fighting to preserve that core ever since, in an almost fascistic way (in the sense that dissent is so bitterly put down, those who disagreed were literally made to feel mentally ill, traitorous, "not really gay" etc.). In the last decade, only because of the tenacity of nonconformists (mostly gay conservatives and republicans), this hegemony was broken and freedom of thought has begun to flourish. The gay political elite was exposed as an ossified dinosaur, and the proliferation of alternative views—and agendas—from all ends of the spectrum has had an enormously positive impact on the representation of gay political aspirations. What used to be termed as "the movement" is now practically nonexistent. There is such a wide and much more representative spectrum of gay political interest groups today, and by that I think it is not accurate to point to the usual suspects in the "gay movement"—with this or that "demand"—as representing our whole community anymore. So, any group which shouts "demands" can do so all it wants, but unless a huge spectrum of diverse groups joins in (and this is increasingly rare) then no one pays much attention. When we do get together with one voice (like on benefits for 9/11 victim partners), we usually win. One group can no longer dictate the agenda—not even HRC—and this is tremendously positive.

The majority of the vocal gay leaders, Log Cabin excepted, are advocates of more government, more programs, more laws. . . . In this regard I believe that some of these demands are too high. For instance, I do not believe in gay marriage. This is my personal view.

Liberal LGBTs

On the other hand, I discovered that only a few liberal LGBTs view gay activist's demands as too demanding and gay activists as being too confrontational. In fact, most liberal LGBTs stated that the LGBT community did not demand enough. For example, in question 6, 7 of the 15 participants, or 46 percent, answered LGBT demands are too low.

A few examples of "too low" responses are as follows:

> It's been too low. The movement is partially splintered but for the most part is united enough to present a strong voice. I would push for more confrontation with misinformed LGBT (mostly gay white males) that vote their pocketbook and ignore their conscience.

> I think groups that follow the model that ACT Out used are not at all necessary currently. It is much better to play by the rules and win within the system as we have done here in a conservative state like X, where four gay democrats have been elected. I don't think we demand too much, but I think our message is at times disjointed.

> No. The LGBT movement is not confrontational enough.

> We are still not doing enough. But, anyone of any orientation within any organization who asks that the laws of our country be administered justly across all persuasions and definitions can hardly be called "confrontational." Society was "confrontational," not Dr. Martin Luther King. To act as if you expect your rights and protections is not confrontational.

> Obviously, LGBT demands are too low. However, there is no clear agenda. Demands of the community should be to be treated as equals in relation to heterosexuals. But, anything that jeopardizes this should be confronted.

Hypothesis 1e

Conservative LGBTs are more likely than liberal LGBTs to not view LGBTs as an oppressed group.

Conservative LGBTs

I found that, for the most part, conservative LGBTs *do not* view LGBTs as an oppressed group. For example, in question 7, 10 of the

15 participants, or 67 percent, did not view LGBTs as an oppressed group.

A few examples of "not oppressed" responses are as follows:

> No, but there are civil rights disparities.

> No. However, we are given unequal treatment by unfair laws—like "Don't Ask, Don't Tell," or state sodomy laws. These are clear targets to press in advancing equal rights for LGBTs.

> Hell no! Our rights accrue to us as individuals. As individuals we have a variety of talents and abilities and opportunities to protect our rights, as well as our collective interests. We aren't enslaved as a group. We aren't denied most of our rights—most of us have places to live, employment, and the basic necessities of life. But it is those gays and lesbians that are most isolated who are at most risk—particularly those young people just discovering their sexuality and just coming out—they need our support as a "community." There needs to be a safety net for them if they have been rejected by their families.

> Not largely, except in some areas of law and policy. In cultural terms, no. Not anymore. We've crossed a line in recent years where this argument can't be made in a national sense. We face some forms of legal discrimination, there are pockets of cultural resistance and bigotry (mostly by geography) and government has too much say in how it interferes in our private lives, but to say we are "oppressed" overall, in a national sense, is laughable. We are an amazingly powerful community in this nation, in relation to our size, with our wealth, our cultural influence, our visibility, and our political clout. We should start ACTING much more according to this reality and put an end to talk of "oppression" because it's a form of self-sabotage.

> No, but I do see some people addressing themselves as victims when they really are product of their own lack of confidence, involvement, and commitment. Alan Schindler, Matthew Shepard, etc., were victims but many of us aren't. If it weren't for the AIDS epidemic this community would have amassed even greater power, wealth, and influence. Yet, with that being said HIV/AIDS did bring the overall community more into national focus.

Liberal LGBTs

On the contrary, I found that for the most part liberal LGBTs *do* view LGBTs as an oppressed group. For example, in question 7, 11 of the 15 participants, or 73 percent, view LGBTs as an oppressed group.

A few examples of "oppressed" responses are as follows:

> Yep and duh?
>
> Yes, but it's subtle. It's getting to be unpopular to not like us, so people have to be "craftier" about how they oppress us. I think we are beginning to witness a revolt to the religious right's totalitarian control of the Republican Party.
>
> Yes, I think it has to do with your definition of oppressed. I think that laws that deny the LGBT to the same protections as all other individuals contribute to some level of legal oppression. However, economically I do not think they are oppressed. The oppression comes in much more subtle ways because of the lack of antidiscrimination and antihate crimes protections.
>
> Certainly, discriminated against, harassed, and oppressed.
>
> We are second class citizens and will continue to be until we are allowed to marry and can then acquire the 1,400 benefits and responsibilities that heterosexuals get when they marry. We are second class citizens until the military decides your sexual orientation means nothing. We are second class citizens when it comes to harassment, employment opportunities, adoption, taxes, etc.
>
> Of course we are oppressed. A white heterosexual male majority runs this country. Any different group is oppressed in American society.

Hypothesis 1f

Conservative LGBTs *do not* feel there is an inherent conflict in being gay and being conservative; yet, liberal LGBTs *do* feel there is an inherent conflict in being gay and being conservative.

Conservative LGBTs

I found that for the most part, conservative LGBTs do not feel there is an inherent conflict in being gay and being conservative. For example, in question 9, 14 of the 15 participants, or 93 percent, did not feel there is an inherent conflict in being gay and being conservative.

A few examples of "no conflict" responses are as follows:

> No.
>
> Absolutely not! This is a very strange question.
>
> It depends on your definition of conservative. If you mean advocating a society based on the literal interpretation of the Bible then yes. If you

mean valuing those institutions, systems, and laws that seem to have contributed to civilization over time and skepticism about swooping those things away, then no it is not incompatible.

No Conservative means conserving everything—rights, resources, people, and values. Our rights as gays and lesbians should be conserved. If there is an inherent "conflict" it is by those who want to impose their view of the world on us, by restricting our rights. Given that that is decidedly NOT a conservative political view, they are the ones who are in conflict—whether they know it or not.

Under my definition of conservative, of course not. But, if I were a Tom Delay conservative, I would be in great conflict all of the time.

No, but I would ask why would one assume that there is a conflict. There is a conflict only if one believes that there must be a linkage between gay equal rights and the host of leftist causes to which it is popular to tie them. It is too often taken for granted that if you are gay you must be antgun, a registered democrat, pro-abortion, opposed to war in Iraq, against school vouchers, etc., etc. In truth, those who see a conflict are guilty of lazy thinking. It's much easier to label a person and then fill the rest of his basket with everything else you just link with that label. Now you don't have to stop to think about what he believes about fiscal policy, the homeless, who to vote for president or the role of the U.S. in Mideast peace negotiations. You don't have to think about him as a person. You've already lumped him into a group. There again, it is a problem of sloppy thinking. Sexual orientation really doesn't really determine anything other than whom you're going to check out at the beach. I would also ask, how can a gay person be a republican? This is a bonus. Probably every gay republican has been asked this question. The answer is not difficult. Both of the two major parties have central tenets and they tend to attract people who align more with one set than the other. Additionally, those who are fiscally conservative, in general, tend to also be socially conservative and a socially conservative person has a higher probability of thinking bad things about gay people. My experience tells me from 10 to 20 percent of those I am going to come into contact with think so poorly of gay people that it colors their political thinking. However, I have a much better chance in converting those 20 percent who disagree with me on gay issues than I do against the 80 percent of the people in the Democratic Party who disagree with me on the fundamental role of government in society.

Liberal LGBTs

On the other hand, I discovered that liberal LGBTs do feel there is an inherent conflict in being gay and being conservative. Of the 15 participants, 9 answered that there is an inherent conflict between being an LGBT and being politically conservative.

A few examples of "conflict" responses are as follows:

> Yes.

> Yes, absolutely. It is an oxymoron in a way. You really have to be self-loathing to be a gay republican.

> Yes, but I see no issue with being spiritually conservative and gay. However, voting for republicans or what is typically viewed, as conservative legislators in the U.S. are not only conflicted, it's insane. LGBTs voting for officials that answer to a faction of the Republican Party that would like to see LGBT eliminated from the U.S. are conflicted. Most gay conservatives are in denial or "self-loathers" and have a poor sense of priorities.

> Yes, but you know what? In many ways and on many issues I am personally conservative and proudly so. However, I find a conflict when one is a republican and gay.

> Absolutely. I cannot believe that any individual who has experienced oppression in any form will then turn around and do the same to others unless they are truly self-hating and self-loathing. And I think that may be the case among many politically conservative gays.

> Unfortunately, yes. The current definition of conservatism is no longer its historical meaning.

> There shouldn't be, but unfortunately, conservative equals republican. And the fact is republicans are just not a friendly crowd towards gays. Thus, philosophically, no I don't think there should be a conflict, but in reality there is.

> Well, technically, yes, but also not necessarily. However, since conservative generally means the acceptance of "traditional" family values and adherence to moral behaviors that conflict with most gay sexual activities, I must say yes. Honestly, I don't know that I could believe that a gay person could categorize themselves as a true conservative without a rather strong degree of self-loathing or denial of what it means to embrace fully those conservative values. I suppose it's all a matter of how any individual defines "conservative" for themselves and their way of life, and how it relates to the commonly held definition of the term.

In the next section, I present the findings from the group consciousness questions. I plan to link both the conservative LGBT and liberal LGBT surveys to the group consciousness theory.

GROUP IDENTITY
AND GROUP CONSCIOUSNESS FINDINGS

Katherine Tate's (1994) *From Protest to Politics: The New Black Voters in American Elections* utilized several questions to understand the group identity and group consciousness of African Americans (p. 93). Also, she used information from the 1984 NBES data to construct measures of both group identification and group consciousness of African Americans. Tate discovers that prosperous African Americans were so adverse to social programs that the phenomena represented a class division within the black community. However, wealthier African Americans were not only opposed to social programs, but also hostile to any aid to minority groups. Tate concludes, "Strong race identifiers" are "African Americans which identify strongly with others of their race are the most inclined to sustain a liberal viewpoint in defiance of their economic status" (p. 22). Thus, I determined Tate's questions on race could be used to examine group consciousness in conservative LGBTs. I used the following questions to construct measures of both group identification and group consciousness of politically active LGBTs.

Group Identity

Common Fate

Detailed data responses are presented in Tables 4.28, 4.29, and 4.30.

1. Do you think what happens generally to LGBTs in this country will have something to do with what happens in your life? (Yes, No) Will it affect you a lot, some, or not very much?
2. Do you think that the movement for LGBT rights has affected you personally? (Yes, No)
3. People differ in whether they think about being LGBT—what they have in common with other LGBT members. What about you— do you think about this a lot, fairly often, once in a while, or hardly ever?

TABLE 4.28. Common fate question 1.

	Conservatives		Liberals	
	#	%	#	%
A lot	4	27	9	60
Some	9	60	5	33
Not very much	2	13	1	7

Note: Of the 15 conservative participants, 4, or 27 percent, answered a lot, 9, or 60 percent, answered some, and 2, or 13 percent, answered not very much. Out of the 15 liberal participants, 9, or 60 percent, answered a lot, 5 or 33 percent, answered some, and 1, or 6 percent, answered not very much.

TABLE 4.29. Common fate questions 2.

	Conservatives		Liberals	
	#	%	#	%
Yes	13	87	15	100
No	2	13	0	0

Note: Of the 15 conservative participants, 9, or 87 percent, answered yes. Of the fifteen participants, 2, or 13 percent, answered no. All 15 liberal participants answered yes.

TABLE 4.30. Common fate question 3.

	Conservatives		Liberals	
	#	%	#	%
A lot	1	7	7	47
Fairly often	2	13	4	27
Once in a while	8	53	3	20
Hardly ever	4	27	1	7

Note: Of the 15 conservative participants, 1, or 7 percent, answered a lot, 2, or 13 percent, answered fairly often, 8, or 53 percent, answered once in a while, and 4, or 27 percent, answered hardly ever. Of the 15 liberal participants, 7, or 47 percent, answered a lot, 4, or 27 percent, answered fairly often, 3, or 20 percent, answered once in a while, and 1, or 7 percent, answered hardly ever.

In summary, although conservative LGBTs might declare to share "common fate" with those of a similar sexual identity, this does not appear to be the case. Clearly, the results of the commonality questions demonstrate that liberal LGBTs are much more likely to see the

TABLE 4.31. Autonomy question 4.

	Conservatives		Liberals	
	#	%	#	%
LGBT	1	7	7	47
Both	4	27	8	53
American	10	67	0	0

Note: In question 4, 1 of the 15 conservative participants, or 7 percent, answered being LGBT, 4, or 27 percent, answered both LGBT and American, and 10, or 67 percent, answered American. Of the 15 liberal participants, 7, or 47 percent, answered an LGBT, 8, or 53 percent, answered both LGBT and American, and none of the 15 participants answered American.

commonality of the entire LGBT community. On the other hand, I might make the assumption that conservative LGBTs' commonality is more associated with those individuals who share a similar class status. Thus, the conservative LGBT sees commonality based on class and not on sexual identity.

LGBT Autonomy

Detailed data responses are presented in Table 4.31.

4. Which is more important, being LGBT, both LGBT and American, or American?
5. LGBTs should not have anything to do with heterosexuals? *Note:* All 30 participants, both conservative and liberal, answered no to this question.

In summary, the autonomy questions demonstrate that liberal LGBTs, much more so than the conservative LGBTs, want an explicit LGBT identity. Also, The conservative LGBTs viewed themselves as Americans versus the liberal LGBTs. In fact, the two groups appear to have opposite opinions on the autonomy issue.

Group Consciousness

Discontent with Group Status

Detailed data responses are presented in Table 4.32.

TABLE 4.32. Discontent with group status.

	Conservatives		Liberals	
	#	%	#	%
Too much	0	0	0	0
Just right	12	80	6	40
Too little	3	20	9	60

Note: Of the 15 conservative participants, 0 answered too much, 12, or 80 percent, answered just right, and 3, or 20 percent, answered too little. Out of the 15 liberal participants, 0 answered too much, 6, or 40 percent, answered just right, 9, or 60 percent, answered too little.

6. Do LGBTs as a group have too much influence, just about the right amount of influence, or too little influence (in American life and politics)?

In summary, the results of the "discontent with group status" question demonstrate that conservative LGBTs are not too worried about the political influence of LGBTs in America. Most conservative LGBTs appear to think the influence of LGBTs is just right. On the other hand, liberal LGBTs believe LGBT influence is too little. Thus, liberal LGBTs are much more discontent with the LGBT group status. This might explain why many liberal LGBTs are willing to participate in radical protests.

Perception of Discrimination

Detailed data responses are presented in Table 4.33.

7. If LGBTs do not do well in life, it is because they are kept back because of their sexuality, or they don't work hard enough to get ahead?

In summary, the perception of discrimination question demonstrates that both groups are split on their views of LGBT discrimination. Most seem to feel LGBTs are held back for both reasons; although, the liberal LGBTs were more likely to say that LGBTs are held back because of their sexual identity.

Support for Collective Strategies

Detailed data responses are presented in Table 4.34.

8. To have power and improve their positions in the United States, LGBTs should be more active in LGBT political organizations; or each LGBT person should work hard to improve his or her own personal situation.

In summary, the "support for collective strategies" question demonstrates that conservative LGBTs believe that individual strategies, such as working hard are more important than collective strategies. On the other hand, liberal LGBTs appear to want to engage in collective strategies by joining political groups.

TABLE 4.33. Perception of discrimination.

	Conservatives		Liberals	
	#	%	#	%
Sexuality	3	20	5	33
Do not work hard	8	53	4	27
Both	4	27	6	40

Note: Of the 15 conservative participants, 3, or 20 percent, answered LGBTs are kept back because of their sexuality, 8, or 53 percent, answered LGBTs do not work hard enough to get ahead, and 4, or 27 percent, answered both. Out of the 15 liberal participants, 5, or 33 percent, answered LGBTs are kept back because of their sexuality, 4, or 27 percent, answered LGBTs do not work hard enough to get ahead, and 6, or 40 percent, answered both.

TABLE 4.34. Support for collective strategies.

	Conservatives		Liberals	
	#	%	#	%
More active	3	20	7	47
Should improve	8	53	3	20
Both	4	27	5	33

Note: Of the 15 conservative participants, 3, or 20 percent, answered LGBTs should be more active in LGBT political organizations, 8, or 53 percent, answered each LGBT person should work hard to improve his or her own personal situation, and 4, or 27 percent, answered both. Of the 15 liberal participants, 7, or 47 percent, answered LGBTs should be more active in LGBT political organizations, 3, or 20 percent, answered each LGBT person should work hard to improve his or her own personal situation, and 5, or 33 percent, answered both.

Group Political Efficacy

Detailed data responses are presented in Table 4.35.

9. If enough LGBTs vote, they can make a difference in who gets elected president. (Agree strongly, Agree somewhat, Disagree somewhat, Disagree strongly?)

In summary, both conservative and liberal LGBTs believe in the strength of political efficacy. Both groups feel their one vote can make a difference. However, this sample is of 30 participants who are politically active in the LGBT community. In fact, most of the participants are presidents of their local republican or democratic LGBT chapters. In light of that, this finding did not surprise me.

Length of Time "Out"

Detailed data responses are presented in Table 4.36.

10. Please state how long you've been "out" to family, friends and co-workers. If not "out" to family, friends, and co-workers, please state "not out."

In summary, the coming-out question demonstrates that conservative LGBTs have not been "out" to family, friends, and co-workers as long as liberal LGBTs. Therefore, I might hypothesize two conclu-

TABLE 4.35. Political efficacy.

	Conservatives		Liberals	
	#	%	#	%
Agree strongly	8	53	9	60
Agree somewhat	7	47	5	33
Disagree somewhat	0	0	1	7
Disagree strongly	0	0	0	0

Note: Of the 15 conservative participants, 8, or 53 percent, answered strongly agree and 7, or 47 percent, answered somewhat agree. Of the 15 liberal participants, 9, or 60 percent, answered strongly agree, 5, or 33 percent, answered somewhat agree, and 1, or 7 percent, answered disagree somewhat.

TABLE 4.36. Length of time out.

	Conocrvalives		Liberals	
	#	%	#	%
One to five	1	7	1	7
Five to ten	7	47	2	13
Ten to twenty	4	27	5	33
Twenty	3	20	7	47
Not out	0	0	0	0

Note: Of the 15 conservative participants, 1, or 6 percent, answered one to five years, 7, or 47 percent, answered five to ten years, 4, or 27 percent, answered ten to twenty years, and 3, or 20 percent, answered twenty or more years. Finally, 0 of the participants answered not out. Of the 15 liberal participants, 1, or 7 percent, answered 1 to 5 years. Of the 15 participants, 2, or 13 percent, answered five to ten years; 5 of the 15 participants, or 33 percent, answered ten to twenty years; and 7 of the 15 participants, or 47 percent, answered twenty or more years. Finally, 0 of the participants answered not out.

sions. First, liberal LGBTs appear to be slightly older than conservative LGBTs. And because of a younger age could conservative LGBTs be less aware of the radical politics of the early 1970s? Next, could it be that conservative LGBTs are not comfortable with their sexual identity yet? Thus, they are less likely to rock the boat or make societal demands.

really? young ppl more radical historically [handwritten annotation]

CONCLUSION

Chapter 4 described group consciousness as part of the LGBT coming-out process. It detailed Cass's four-stage LGBT group identity process. Finally, the chapter ended with a short survey of both leading conservative and liberal LGBT. Overall, Chapter 4 explained that conservative LGBTs do not see a need to group identify with their sexual identity and identify with some other variable. In fact, Chapter 5 will investigate whether conservative LGBTs are group identifying with other variables, such as class and social and/or economic status.

Chapter 5

LGBT Conservative Identity:
Presentation of Data

The purpose of this examination was the analysis of "group identity" in relation to conservative LGBTs. Group theory, as mentioned in Chapter 2, states that individuals who join political groups are motivated by shared interests and disturbances and crises play a role in group formation. Specifically, the study observed conservative LGBTs who might be part of the assimilation movement. Thus, the individuals had to self-identify as a member of the conservative LGBT group. However, it is necessary to examine the specific characteristics of conservative LGBTs. In other words, I ask "What variables make a conservative LGBT different from a liberal LGBT"?

In order to find such individuals, I utilized an online LGBT survey conducted by Harris Interactive for the Gill Foundation from November 30 to December 5, 2000. Overall, the survey found that 10 percent of LGBTs self-identified with conservative political philosophies. I then examined those LGBT members who identified as being members of the conservative group. However, the self-selected nature of the sample raises the possibility that younger, male, and Caucasian individuals are overrepresented in the sample. This, too, reflects the difficulty in trying to sample the LGBT community. More information on dilemmas involved in investigations on the LGBT population can be found in the studies by Warren (1974).

Harris Interactive based the original data analysis on completed post-2000 election online questionnaires of 1,146 LGBTs conducted for the Gill Foundation from November 30 through December 5, 2000. I wish to examine those 10 percent of LGBT individuals who self-identified as conservative producing a sample of 118 LGBT individu-

Gay Conservatives: Group Consciousness and Assimilation
© 2007 by The Haworth Press, Inc. All rights reserved.
doi:10.1300/5722_05

als. My examination of the self-identified liberal LGBT produced a
sample of 495. This data was taken from question 220 of the completed post 2000 election online questionnaire that asked LGBT individuals to describe their own political philosophy (Figure 5.1). However, it must be stressed that it is difficult to obtain a random sample
of the LGBT community, and especially of closeted LGBT individuals. The problem of the "closet" and the apprehension of self-disclo-
sure of the LGBT community often create concerns about LGBT
sample validity. Many LGBT individuals fear divulgence of their
sexual self-identity as well as their personal and political beliefs.
Hence, the Harris Poll provides an excellent source for sampling
LGBT opinion because it offers confidentiality and anonymity for individuals, thereby protecting their sexual identity.

Online research is occasionally labeled as "convenience sampling" because it is grounded on individuals choosing to participate
in survey research. Therefore, the survey participants are not ran-
domly selected from a cross-section of the population. This self-
selection can misconstrue and distort the data, which may result in
both predictable and unpredictable biases in the model. Also, I spoke
with someone at Harris's Claremont office who specifically stated

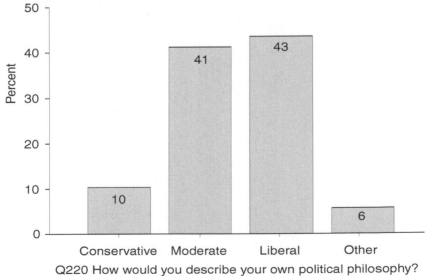

FIGURE 5.1. Political philosophy.

that the online survey method did still suffer from an over bias of young Caucasian males. Finally, online surveys do not fairly represent those populations who have limited access to the Internet. Thus, online samples often distort the data with individuals who possess higher degrees of both income and education. Particularly, this study had a high degree of young male respondents. Most likely, it reflects that younger men are more comfortable utilizing online technology and expressing their sexual identity.

Other possible survey methods are face-to-face interviews or random telephone techniques, but this can be very costly and time consuming, although neither method guarantees a genuinely reliable cross section of the population. Also, given this study's need to have a higher sample of LGBT individuals, the study would most likely have to rely on LGBT marketing data to reach urban areas with higher concentrations of LGBT individuals. Overall, the research mission is to achieve a purposive sample, where LGBT members demonstrate adequate divergence on the major variables being investigated.

The principal pattern of data analysis utilized was broken into three sections. First, a descriptive comparison was developed to analyze the 118 conservative LGBTs. Next, a cross-tabulation was used to compare conservative LGBTs and liberal LGBTs. Last, I developed an examination of determinants of these differences using binary regression models. This policy was followed since I could determine no natural breaks in the distribution of responses for many variables. Thus, throughout my study, unless indicated otherwise, the sample size was 118. In addition, I used the SPSS programs to investigate and chart data.

DESCRIPTIVE DIFFERENCES

Tables 5.1 and 5.2 provide an overview of conservative LGBT characteristics. Older, white males of higher socioeconomic status are somewhat over represented in the sample as a whole, but this is not unexpected, given the online survey technique used to gather the original LGBT data. Of conservative LGBTs, 66 percent was identified as male. This corresponds to the total LGBT sample of which 66 percent

TABLE 5.1. Overall characteristics of respondents (Interactive Harris) data.

	LGBTs	Conservative LGBTs	Liberal LGBTs
Means			
Age	41.9	42.9	41.5
Education	5.80	5.46	5.89
Income	6.29	6.03	6.27
Percentages			
Male	64.0%	66.1%	61.2%
White	77.0%	92.4%	86.1%
Married	22.0%	35.6%	12.1%
Christian	18.0%	29.7%	12.0%
Employed	62.0%	64.4%	60.4%
Sample size (unweighted)	1,146	118	495

TABLE 5.2. Descriptive statistics of conservative LGBTs.

	N	Mean	Std. Deviation
Sex	118	2.3390	.47538
Age	118	42.9407	12.97222
Education	118	5.4576	1.15206
Household income	118	6.0254	2.87477
Marriage status	118	4.1186	2.17275
Religious preferences	118	9.0932	5.66438
Race	118	2.3390	1.34113
Employed full-time	118	.6441	.48084
Employed part-time	118	.0339	.18174
Self employed	118	.0932	.29198
Not employed, but looking	118	.0424	.20230
Not employed, not looking	118	.0169	.12963
Retired	118	.1441	.35266
Student	118	.0763	.26656
Homemaker	118	.0763	.26656
Valid *N*	118		

of LGBTs also identified as male. Of conservative LGBTs, 36 were between the ages of 35 and 44. However, 50 percent of the total LGBT sample identified between the ages of 18 and 34. I determined that the average age for conservative LGBTs was 42.9. Of conservative LGBTs, 40 percent identified as having some college education, but only 27 percent of the total sample of LGBTs identified as having some college education. In fact, the conservative LGBT averaged 5.46 (the number 5 equaled some college education) for education. Of the conservative LGBTs, 43 percent identified having household incomes of greater than $50K, whereas 38 percent of the total LGBT sample identified having household incomes of greater than $50K. In fact, the conservative LGBT averaged 6.03 (the number 6 equaled incomes ranging from $50K to $75K) for household income. Of conservative LGBTs, 36 percent identified as being married, whereas only 22 percent of the total LGBT sample identified as being married. Of conservative LGBTs, 30 percent identified as Christian, with 23 percent of the total LGBT sample identified as Christian. Finally, the vast majority of the sample, 92 percent of conservative LGBTs identified as white, whereas 74 percent of the total LGBT sample identified as white.

DESCRIPTIVE STATISTICS

Figures 5.2 through 5.9 provide further information on subpopulations of the sample divided by age, sex, race, education, relationships, household income, employment, and religious choice. Conservative LGBTs are identified by .00 and liberal LGBTs are identified by 1.00.

Age

Summary comparisons of age-related difference for the sample (Figure 5.2) demonstrate a cross-tabulation (Appendix) of age with over 44 percent of conservatives LGBTs over the age of 45. On the other hand, 40 percent of liberal LGBT identified as being

Percentages	Conservative LGBTs	Liberal LGBTs	Other LGBTs
18-34	26.3	32.3	28.3
35-44	29.7	27.5	31.0
45-54	23.7	23.2	23.6
55+	20.3	17.0	17.1
Total	100	100	100

$\chi^2 = .135$, $p < .05$

Descriptive Statistics

Ideology		N	Minimum	Maximum	Mean	Std. Deviation
Other	Age	533	18.00	78.00	42.0788	12.52657
	Valid N (listwise)	533				
Liberal	Age	495	17.00	74.00	41.4687	12.67000
	Valid N (listwise)	495				
Conservatives	Age	118	19.00	73.00	42.9407	12.97222
	Valid N (listwise)	118				

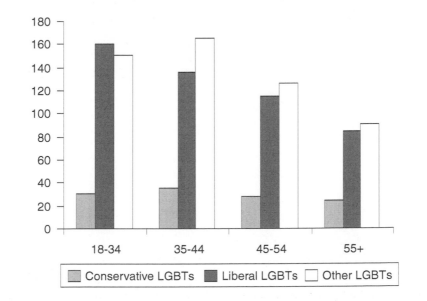

FIGURE 5.2. Response to age (in percent).

over the age of 45. Thus, greater proportions of LGBT conservatives are older than LGBT liberals. The results can be summarized as follows:

1. Of the older conservative LGBTs (45+), 53 percent are male, whereas 47 percent of younger conservative LGBTs (under 45) are male. Thus, conservative male LGBTs are more likely to be older than younger conservative LGBTs.
2. Of the older conservative LGBTs (45+), 55 percent have graduated college, whereas 45 percent of younger conservative LGBTs (under 45) have graduated college. Hence, younger conservative LGBTs are not as highly educated.
3. Of the older conservative LGBTs (45+), 45 percent of the older conservative LGBTs (45+) have household incomes of $50K or more, whereas 55 percent of younger conservative LGBTs (under 45) have household incomes greater than $50K.
4. Of the older conservative LGBTs (45+), another 50 percent identified as married, whereas 50 percent of younger conservative LGBTs (under 45) identified as married.
5. Of the older conservative LGBTs (45+), 41 percent identified as religious, whereas 59 percent of the younger conservative LGBTs (under 45) identified as religious.
6. Of the older conservative LGBTs (45+), 45 percent identified as white, whereas 45 percent of the younger conservative LGBT (under 45) identified as white.

Gender

Summary comparisons of gender-related difference for the sample (Figure 5.3) demonstrate a cross-tabulation of sex (Appendix), with 66 percent of conservative LGBTs identifying as male and 34 percent of conservative LGBTs identifying as females. This corresponds exactly to the total LGBT sample of 1,146. However, 61 percent of liberal LGBTs identified as male and 38 percent of liberal

Percentages	Conservative LGBTs	Liberal LGBTs	Other LGBTs
Male	66.1	61.2	66.0
Female	33.9	38.4	33.4
Other	00.0	00.4	00.6
Total	100	100	100

$\chi^2 = .508, p < .05$

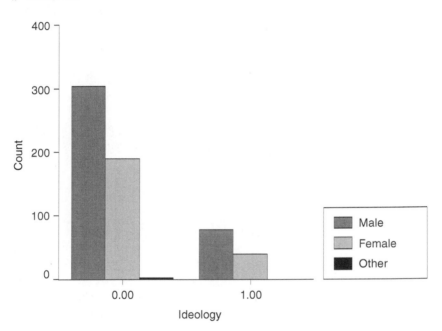

FIGURE 5.3. Response to gender (in percent).

LGBTs identified as females. The results can be summarized as follows:

1. Of conservative LGBT males, 79 percent are 45 years of age. However, 21 percent of conservative LGBT females are over 45. Therefore, conservative LGBTs tend to be medium-aged males and younger-aged females.
2. Of conservative LGBT males, 82 percent have graduated college, whereas only 18 percent of conservative LGBT females

have graduated college. Hence, conservative LGBT females are not as highly educated as the conservative LGBT males.

3. Of conservative LGBT males, 65 percent have household incomes of $50K or more whereas only 35 percent of conservative LGBT females have household incomes greater than $50K. Thus, conservative LGBT males make more money than conservative LGBT females.

4. Of conservative LGBT males, 62 percent have identified as married, whereas only 38 percent of conservative LGBT females identified as married. Therefore, more conservative LGBT males identified as married than females.

5. Of conservative LGBT males, 65 percent identified as religious whereas 35 percent of conservative LGBT females identified as religious.

6. Of conservative LGBT males, 67 percent identified as white, whereas 33 percent of the conservative LGBT females identified as white.

Race

A summary comparison of race-related difference for the sample (Figure 5.4) demonstrates a cross-tabulation of race (Appendix), with 92 percent of conservative LGBTs self-identifying as white. Of the total LGBT sample of 1,146, 74 percent self-identified as white and 16 percent self-identified as African American. However, 86 percent of liberal LGBTs identified as being white.

1. Of the conservative LGBT males, 94 percent identified as white, and 90 percent of the conservative LGBT females identified as white. Hence, the number of conservative LGBT males who identified white as their race was slightly more than the number of females. Interestingly, in the sample, 1 percent of both conservative LGBT males and females self-identified as African American. The study additionally produced findings of 1 percent conservative LGBT males who identified as American Indian and 1 percent conservative LGBT females who identified as Asian.

2. The largest age group of conservative LGBTs (44 percent) self-identifying as white was over the age of 45. In fact, each age group had large percentage of conservatives LGBTs self-identifying as white. Clearly, white conservative LGBTs are of all ages.
3. Of conservative LGBTs self-identifying as white, 98 percent have graduated college. Another 88 percent self-identifying as white did not graduate college. African-American conservative LGBTs have only graduated high school and conservative LGBTs in only one of the other races have graduated college.
4. Of the conservative LGBTs self-identifying as white, 94 percent have household incomes of $50K or more. The 1 percent of conservative LGBTs self-identifying as African American have household incomes under $50K. Also, 1 percent of conservative LGBTs self-identifying as Asian and other have household incomes ranging between $50K and $75K.
5. Of conservative LGBTs self-identifying as white, 86 percent also identified as married. Also, 1 percent of conservative LGBTs self-identifying as African American, Asian, and other also identified as married. However, another 95 percent of conservative LGBTs self-identifying as white indicated that they were nonmarried.
6. Of conservative LGBTs self-identifying as white, 77 percent also identified as being religious. The 4 percent of conservative LGBTs self-identifying as African American, Asian, and other also described themselves as being religious.

Education

Summary comparisons of education-related differences for the sample (Figure 5.5) demonstrate a cross-tabulation of education (Appendix) with 70 percent of conservative LGBTs self-identifying as having some college education. Of the total LGBT sample of 1,146, 45 percent identified as having some college education. However, 92 percent of liberal LGBTs identified as having some college education or more. Therefore, liberal LGBTs are more highly educated than conservative LGBTs and the general LGBT population.

Percentages	Conservative LGBTs	Liberal LGBTs	Other LGBTs
White	92.4	86.1	00.7
African American	01.7	02.4	02.0
Asian	00.0	00.8	01.5
Native American	00.0	02.6	01.1
Mixed background	00.0	02.8	03.6
Other	03.4	01.8	01.7
Decline to answer	02.5	03.5	03.4
Total	100	100	100

$\chi^2 = .664$, $p < .05$

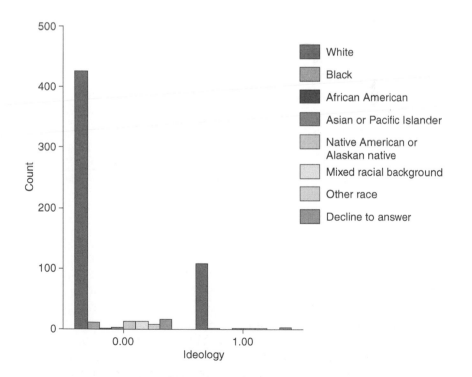

FIGURE 5.4. Response to race (in percent).

Percentages	Conservative LGBTs	Liberal LGBTs	Other LGBTs
Some high school	03.4	01.8	02.3
High school graduate	13.6	6.50	09.9
Some college	39.8	37.8	35.8
College graduate	27.1	26.1	25.5
Some graduate school	09.3	09.9	11.3
Graduate school graduate	06.8	18.0	15.2
Total	100	100	100

$\chi^2 = .008$, $p < .05$.

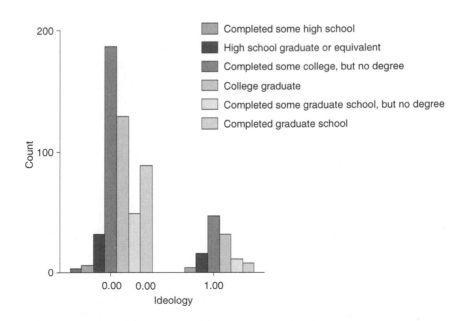

FIGURE 5.5. Response to education (in percent).

1. Of conservative LGBT males, 86 percent have graduated college whereas 22 percent of conservative LGBT females have graduated college. Hence, conservative LGBT females are not as educated as the conservative LGBT males.
2. Of the older conservative LGBTs (45+), 54 percent have graduated college, whereas only 46 percent of younger conservative LGBTs (under 45) have graduated college. Hence, younger conservative LGBTs are not as highly educated as older conservative LGBTs.
3. Of conservative LGBTs self-identifying as white, 46 percent have graduated college, whereas 54 percent have not. African-American conservative LGBTs have graduated only high school. Also, only 1 percent of conservative LGBTs in the other races have graduated college.
4. Only 49 percent of conservative LGBTs, who have graduated college, have household incomes over $50K.
5. Of conservative LGBTs who have graduated college, 33 percent identified as being married.
6. Of conservative LGBTs who have graduated college, 46 percent identified as being a member of some religion.

Relationships

Summary comparisons of marital-related difference for the sample (Figure 5.6) demonstrate a cross-tabulation of relationships (Appendix) with 36 percent of conservative LGBTs self-identifying as being married and 33 percent identifying as being partnered. Of the total LGBT sample of 1,146, 22 percent identified as being married and 34 percent identified as being partnered. Of the liberal LGBTs identified as being married 12 percent and another 37 percent identified as being partnered. Therefore, conservative LGBTs are much more likely to be married, but slightly less likely to be partnered than the LGBT population. This study is only going to examine the marriage phenomena in the cross-tabulations because of the unique quality of a LGBT individual to be married. Specifically, question 135 asks the individual to clarify whether he or she is married or in a civil union. Thus, many of the conservative LGBTs are in a male-female marriage.

Percentages	Conservative LGBTs	Liberal LGBTs	Other LGBTs
Married	35.6	12.1	22.1
Single	21.2	38.8	35.6
Divorced*	06.8	07.7	06.8
Separated	01.7	01.0	02.6
Widowed	01.7	01.2	01.7
Living with partner	33.1	37.4	30.4
Civil union	00.0	01.8	00.8
Total	100	100	100

$\chi^2 = .000$, $p < .05$.

*Includes divorce from civil unions.

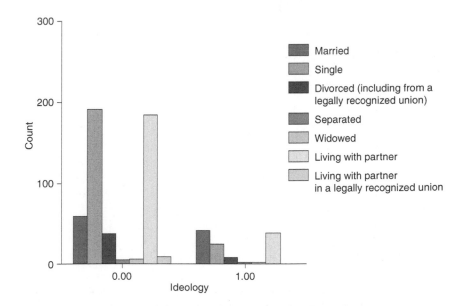

FIGURE 5.6. Response to partner status (in percent).

1. Of the conservative LGBT males, 62 percent have identified as married. But only 38 percent of conservative LGBT females identified as married. Therefore, more conservative LGBT males identified as married than females.
2. Another 40 percent of the older conservative LGBTs (45+) identified as married, whereas 32 percent of younger conservative LGBTs (under 45) identified as married. With these results, it is unclear which conservative LGBT age group would be more likely to be married.
3. Of conservative LGBTs who have graduated college, 27 percent identified as being married.
4. Of conservative LGBTs self-identifying as white, 33 percent also identified as married. Also, 83 percent of conservative LGBTs self-identifying as African American, Asian, and other also described themselves as married. An additional 32 percent of conservative LGBTs self-identifying as white indicated they were not married.
5. Of conservative LGBTs self-identifying as married, 43 percent had household incomes greater than $50K a year.
6. Of conservative LGBTs self-identifying as married, 37 percent also identified as being religious.

Religion

Summary comparisons of religion-related difference for the sample (Figure 5.7) demonstrate a cross-tabulation of religion (Appendix) with 84 percent of conservative LGBTs self-identifying as being a member of some religion. Of the total LGBT sample of 1,146, 73 percent identified as being a member of some religion. Therefore, conservative LGBTs are much more likely to be a member of some religion. However, it was also discovered that 75 percent of liberal LGBTs identified as being a member of some religion.

1. Of conservative LGBT males, 82 percent identified as being a member of some religion, and 88 percent of conservative LGBT females identified as being a member of some religion.

2. Of older conservative LGBTs (45+), 96 percent identified as being a member of some religion, and 88 percent of younger conservative LGBTs (under 45) identified as being member of some religion.
3. Of conservative LGBTs who reported having some college education, 90 percent additionally self-identified as being a member of some religion.
4. Of conservative LGBTs who have household incomes above $50K, 94 percent also identified as being a member of some religion.
5. Of conservative LGBTs self-identifying as married, 88 percent also identified as being a member of some religion.
6. Of conservative LGBTs self-identifying as white, 83 percent also identified as being a member of some religion. Also, the 83 percent of conservative LGBTs self-identifying as African American, Asian, and others described themselves as being a member of some religion.

Household Income

Summary comparisons of household income-related difference for the sample (Figure 5.8) demonstrate a cross-tabulation of household income with 43 percent of conservative LGBTs self-identifying as having a household income greater than $50K. Of the total LGBT sample of 1,146, 36 percent identified as having a household income greater than $50K. Therefore, conservative LGBTs are more likely to have a household income greater than $50K. However, 42 percent of liberal LGBT identified as having a household income greater than $50K.

Full-Time Employment

Summary comparisons of employment and student-related difference for the sample (Figure 5.9) demonstrate that 64 percent of conservative LGBTs are more likely to be employed full-time, rather than part-time. Of the total LGBT sample of 1,146, 57 percent identified as being employed full-time. Roughly and 3 percent of conservative LGBTs identified as being part-time employed, whereas 11 per-

	Conservative LGBTs	Liberal LGBTs	Other LGBTs
Buddhist	00.0	00.0	01.1
Catholic	17.8	11.9	17.1
Christian	29.7	12.1	20.1
Mormon	1.7	00.2	00.2
Greek Orthodox	00.8	00.4	00.8
Hindu	00.0	00.2	00.4
Jewish	00.0	00.4	2.10
Islam	00.0	00.0	00.2
Native American	00.8	01.2	00.9
Protestant	17.8	09.3	16.3
Wicca	02.5	05.7	04.3
Agnostic	05.9	10.1	07.1
Atheist	01.7	08.1	03.2
Other	5.10	11.1	09.2
None	11.9	19.0	13.1
Decline to answer	04.2	04.4	03.9
Total	100	100	100

$\chi^2 = .000$, $p < .05$

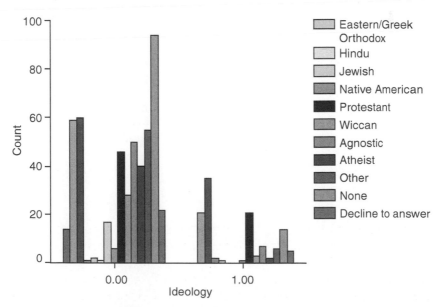

FIGURE 5.7. Response to religion (in percent).

	Conservative LGBTs	Liberal LGBTs	Other LGBTs
Less than $15,000	05.1	07.1	6.19
$15,000 to $24,999	11.9	08.7	9.19
$25,000 to $34,999	10.2	14.5	13.9
$35,000 to $49,999	18.6	17.2	13.5
$50,000 to $74,999	28.0	17.8	19.5
$75,000 to $99,999	11.0	10.7	13.3
$100,000 to $124,999	03.4	04.4	06.8
$125,000 to $149,999	00.8	04.0	02.6
$150,000 to $199,999	00.0	02.8	02.3
$200,000 to $249,999	00.0	01.6	00.9
$250,000 or more	00.0	00.8	00.9
Decline to answer	11.0	10.3	10.9
Total	100	100	100

$\chi c^2 = .097$, $p < .05$

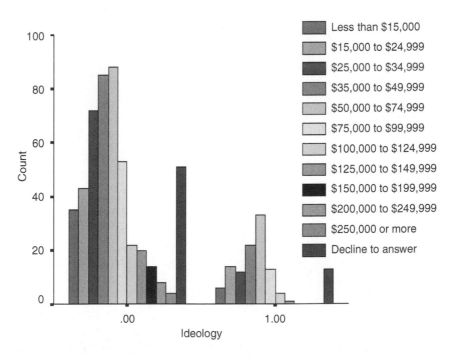

FIGURE 5.8. Response to household income (in percent).

Percentages	Conservative LGBTs	Liberal LGBTs	Other LGBTs
Employed full-time	64.4	60.4	63.6
Employed part-time	3.4	8.9	7.5
Other	32.2	30.7	28.9
Total	100	100	100

$\chi^2 = .423, p < .05$

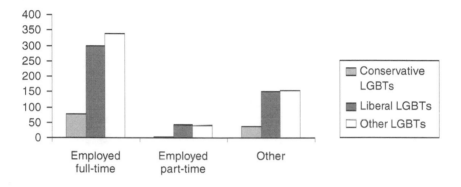

FIGURE 5.9. Response to employment (in percent).

cent of the LGBT sample identified as being employed part-time. Of conservative LGBTs, 7 percent identified as being a student, whereas 13 percent of the total LGBT sample of 1,146 identified as being a student. Therefore, conservative LGBTs are much more likely to be employed full-time than LGBT.

BINARY REGRESSION RESULTS

Table 5.3 details the determinants of the binary regression differences between conservative and liberal LGBTs. Table 5.4 reflects binary regression results from my heterosexual calculation and Table 5.5 illustrates my binary regression results from my general population calculation. The main calculation was a binary regression of the variables. The dependent variable is coded 0 for conservative and 1 for liberal. First, I used a beta calculation to determine the net effect that the dependent variable will change the independent vari-

TABLE 5.3. Variables in the equation—Binary regression differences.

		B	S.E.	Sig.	Exp(B)
Step 1(a)	MIDDLE	.122	.301	.685	1.130
	MIDOLD	−.085	.326	.794	.919
	OLD	.170	.351	.628	1.185
	FEMALE	−.422	.247	.088	.656
	BLACK	−.736	.895	.411	.479
	ASIAN	−1.397	.798	.080	.247
	MIXRAC	−.484	.793	.541	.616
	OTHERAC	−1.372	.662	.038*	.253
	COLLSOME	−.527	.365	.149	.591
	COLLGRAD	−.702	.393	.074	.496
	GRADSCH	−1.163	.420	.006**	.313
	NONMARRY	−1.581	.304	.000**	.206
	PARTNER	−1.313	.295	.000**	.269
	NONEREL	−1.118	.244	.000**	.327
	FULLTIME	.170	.247	.491	1.185
	LESS50	−.253	.396	.523	.776
	MORE50	−.028	.411	.946	.972
	MORE100	−1.679	.620	.007**	.187
	Constant	1.181	.585	.044	3.257

χ^2 = 91.603

Log likelihood = 508.20

Cox and Snell R^2 = .139

* significant at 5% level; ** significant at 1% level

able. Next, I used the Odds Ratio using Euler's constant raised to the power Bi to determine a change in probability. Last, I only examined those variables that demonstrated statistical significance.

Binary Regression of Age

I recoded the age variables into four groups. First, I recoded ages 18 to 34 as young, ages 35 to 44 as middle, ages 45 to 54 as middle/old, and 55 or more as old. In order to create the dummy variables I removed the young group from my regression. Also, the coefficient on middle/old variable shows the change in ideology as people move

TABLE 5.4. Variables in the equation—Heterosexual binary regression results.

		B	S.E.	Sig.	Exp(B)
Step 1(a)	MIDDLE	.609	.098	.000**	1.839
	MIDOLD	.322	.088	.000**	1.379
	OLD	.583	.092	.000**	1.791
	FEMALE	−1.105	.066	.000**	.331
	BLACK	−1.172	.211	.000**	.310
	ASIAN	−.438	.224	.050*	.645
	MIXRAC	−.664	.212	.002**	.515
	OTHERAC	−.198	.143	.166	.820
	COLLSOME	.031	.096	.748	1.031
	COLLGRAD	−.080	.105	.445	.923
	GRADSCH	−.694	.106	.000**	.499
	NONMARRY	−.594	.070	.000**	.552
	PARTNER	−.697	.153	.000**	.498
	NONEREL	−1.525	.078	.000**	.218
	FULLTIME	−.126	.066	.058	.882
	LESS50	−.088	.090	.332	.916
	MORE50	−.078	.093	.400	.925
	MORE100	−.163	.122	.181	.849
	Constant	1.902	.141	.000	6.700

χ^2 = 1117.137

Log likelihood = 6421.694

Cox and Snell R^2 = .168

* significant at 5% level; ** significant at 1% level

from young to middle/old. Overall, I found that none of my age variables appears to be statistically significant for my LGBT population. Yet, both my general population and heterosexual sample demonstrated statistical significance with .000 calculations. If I break down the variables by age groups I get the following results.

Middle Age (35 to 44)

An LGBT person who is between the ages of 35 and 44 is 1.130 times more likely to be conservative. My heterosexual sample between

TABLE 5.5. Variables in the equation—General population binary regression results.

		B	S.E.	Sig.	Exp(B)
Step 1(a)	MIDDLE	.492	.087	.000**	1.635
	MIDOLD	.288	.080	.000**	1.333
	OLD	.620	.084	.000**	1.859
	FEMALE	−.873	.059	.000**	.418
	BLACK	−1.045	.197	.000**	.352
	ASIAN	−.506	.195	.010**	.603
	MIXRAC	−.654	.197	.001**	.520
	OTHERAC	−.133	.127	.295	.876
	COLLSOME	−.064	.088	.463	.938
	COLLGRAD	−.177	.096	.065	.838
	GRADSCH	−.770	.097	.000**	.463
	NONMARRY	−.810	.063	.000**	.445
	PARTNER	−1.472	.112	.000**	.229
	NONEREL	−1.514	.069	.000**	.220
	FULLTIME	−.090	.061	.137	.914
	LESS50	−.122	.083	.139	.885
	MORE50	−.093	.086	.280	.911
	MORE100	−.258	.112	.021*	.772
	Constant	1.836	.129	.000	6.270

$\chi^2 = 1521.322$

Log likelihood = 7676.478

Cox and Snell $R^2 = .194$

* significant at 5% level; ** significant at 1% level

the ages of 35 and 44 is 1.839 times more likely to be conservative. On the other hand, the general population demonstrated 1.635 times more likely to be conservative.

Middle/Old Age (45 to 54)

An LGBT person who is between the ages of 45 and 54 is .919 times more likely to be conservative. My heterosexual sample between the ages of 45 and 54 is 1.379 times more likely to be conservative. On the other hand, the general population between the ages of 45 and 54 was 1.333 times more likely to be conservative.

Old Age (55+)

An LGBT person who is 55 years old or more is 1.185 times more likely to be conservative. My heterosexual sample of 55 or more is 1.791 times more likely to be conservative. On the other hand, the general population of 55 or more demonstrated that it was 1.859 times more likely to be conservative.

Binary Regression of Gender

I only recoded the gender variable for the female group. I did this because I do not need a dummy variable when there are only two choices, such as male or female. Overall, I found that none of my gender variables appears to be statistically significant for my LGBT population. But I did calculate that sample was marginal statistically significant at .088. Furthermore, both my general population and heterosexual sample demonstrated statistical significance with .000 calculations. If I break down the variables by gender groups I get the following results.

Females

An LGBT female is less than .656 times more likely to be conservative. My heterosexual sample showed females are less than .331 times more likely to be conservative. Finally, my general population demonstrates that females are less than .418 times more likely to be conservative. This supports current political behavior literature (Kaufmann and Petrocik 1999), which suggests men are more likely to be conservative than women.

Binary Regression of Race

I recoded the race variables into five groups: white, African American, Asian, mixed race, and other race. In order to create dummy variables, I removed the white group from my regression. I removed the white group because I believed it to be the most obvious group to be conservative. Also, whites have no class obligation that other groups appear to demonstrate (Dawson 1994). My LGBT African-American sample calculation was not statistically significant at .411.

However, both my heterosexual sample and general population were statistically significant at .000. My Asian LGBT sample calculation was marginally statistically significant at .080. Both heterosexual sample and general population were statistically significant at .050 and .010 respectively. My mixed race LGBT calculation was not statistically significant at .541. However, both my heterosexual sample and general population were statistically significant at .002 and .001 respectively. However, my other race calculation *is* statistically significant because its measure is less than .05 at .038. However, other race *is not* statistically significant for either my heterosexual sample at .166, or my general population at .295. If I break down the variables by race groups I obtain the following results.

African American

An LGBT African American is .479 times less likely to be conservative. My heterosexual sample shows an African American is .310 times less likely to be conservative. Finally, my general population demonstrates an African American is .352 times less likely to be conservative.

Asian

An LGBT Asian is .247 times less likely to be conservative. My heterosexual sample shows an Asian is .645 times less likely to be conservative. Finally, my general population demonstrates an Asian is .603 times less likely to be conservative. Although these findings do correspond to the political behavior literature that suggests that Asian Americans generally vote for the Republicans, this voting behavior is not stable over time. In fact, research shows Asian immigrants initially identify as Republican. However, subsequent generations do not develop a specific party identification (Cain, Kiewiet, and Uhlaner 1991).

Mixed Race

An LGBT mixed race is .616 times less likely to be conservative. My heterosexual sample shows that a mixed race is .515 times less likely to be conservative. Finally, my general population demonstrates a mixed race is .520 times less likely to be conservative.

Other Race

An LGBT other race is .253 times less likely to be conservative. My heterosexual sample shows other race is .820 times less likely to be conservative. Finally, my general population demonstrates other race is .876 times less likely to be conservative.

Binary Regression of Education

It is believed that as years of education increases, identification with the Republican Party climbs (Campbell et al. 1980); although it also appears that a graduate school education benefits the Democratic Party a bit and therefore the split narrows. I recoded the education variables into three groups. I recoded some high school and "high school graduate" as college none, some college as college some, college graduate as college graduate, and I recoded some graduate school and graduate school as graduate school. In order to create dummy variables, I removed the college none group from my regression. I removed the college none group because I believed it to be the most obvious group to be conservative. None of my some college LGBT heterosexual and general population calculations was statistically significant at .149, .748, and .463, respectively. My college graduate LGBT and my general population calculations are marginally statistically significant at .074 and .065, respectively. However, heterosexual calculation was not statistically significant. Finally, my graduate school calculation was statistically significant at .006, 000, and .000, respectively, for all three groups. If I break down the variables by education groups I obtain the following results.

Some College

An LGBT person who has some college education is .591 times less likely to be conservative. My heterosexual sample shows a person who has some college education is 1.031 times more likely to be conservative. Finally, my general population demonstrates a person who has some college education is .938 less likely to be conservative.

College Graduate

An LGBT person who has a college education is .496 times less likely to be conservative. My heterosexual sample shows a person who has a college education is .923 times less likely to be conservative. Finally, my general population demonstrates a person with a college education is .838 less likely to be conservative.

Graduate School

An LGBT person who has some graduate school education is .313 times less likely to be conservative. My heterosexual sample shows a person who has some graduate school education is .499 times less likely to be conservative. Finally, my general population demonstrates a person who has some graduate education is .463 less likely to be conservative. However, most likely the graduate and professional degrees were combined. If the professional degrees, such as an MBA, were separated I might have more conservatives.

Binary Regression of Relationship Status

I recoded the relationship variables into three groups. I recoded married as married, single, divorced, separated, and widowed as nonmarried, and partnered and partnered in civil unions as partnered. In order to create dummy variables I removed the married group from my regression. Proof of the marriage gap is found in a study that determined that married people vote 10 to 15 percent more for Republicans than their unmarried counterparts (Weisburg 1987). Thus, I believed that most married gays would be conservative. Overall, I found that relationship does appear to have an impact on change in ideology for the LGBT population in two areas: nonmarried and partnerships. First, the nonmarried calculation was statistically significant at .000, .000, and .000. Next, the partnered calculation was statistically significant at .000, .000, and .000 for all three groups. If I break down the variables by relationship groups I get the following results.

Nonmarried

An LGBT person who is nonmarried is .206 times less likely to be conservative. My heterosexual sample shows that a person who is nonmarried is .552 times less likely to be conservative. Finally, my general population demonstrates a person who is nonmarried is .445 times less likely to be conservative. Again, this makes sense, because single people and widows are most likely to vote Democratic.

Partnered

An LGBT person who is partnered is .269 times less likely to be conservative. My heterosexual sample shows person who is partnered is .498 times less likely to be conservative. Finally, my general population demonstrates a person who is partnered is .229 times less likely to be conservative. This is where the LGBT population statistically appeared to be much different from the heterosexual population. Married Heterosexual are traditionally more conservative. On the other hand, it appears LGBT partnerships are more liberal. It should be noted, however, that this research was conducted before the LGBT community began traditional marriage ceremonies in 2004.

Binary Regression of Religion

I recoded the age variables into seven groups. I recoded Buddhist as Buddha, Hindu as Hindu, Jewish as Jewish, Protestant as Prost, Catholic, Christian, Church of Jesus, and Greek Orthodox as Christian, I recoded other religions as other, and last, I recoded no religious preferences as none religious. In order to create dummy variables I removed the Christian group from my regression. Recent studies show conservative Catholics and conservative Protestants are voting more for the Republican Party (Manza and Brooks 1997). However, my original binary regression did not show much significance with religious choice. So I reran the regression but only using my none religious variable. My none religious calculation was statistically significant at .000, .000, and .000 for all three groups. If I break down the variables by religion groups I obtain the following results.

None Religious

An LGBT person who is none religious is .327 times more likely to be conservative. My heterosexual sample shows a person who is none religious is .218 times less likely to be conservative. Finally, my general population demonstrates a person who is nonreligious is .220

times less likely to be conservative. From this result I can conclude that the LGBT population is slightly less liberal than the heterosexual population in terms of nonreligious.

Binary Regression of Household Income

I recoded the household income variables into four groups. I recoded income less than $50K as less than 50, household income more than $50K but less than $100K as more than 50, household income more than $100K as more than 100, and household income no response as NORES. In order to create dummy variables, I removed the no response group from my regression. My less than $50K calculation was not statistically significant at .523, .332, and .139, respectively for all three groups. In addition, my more than $50K calculation was not statistically significant at .946, .400, and .280, respectively, for all three groups. Next, my more than $100K calculation was statistically significant at .007 and .021 for both my LGBT sample and general population. It is theorized that Democratic support decreases consistently as one ascends the income scale (Campbell et al. 1980).

Overall, I found that household income does have much of an impact on change in ideology for the LGBT population, but only at a high-income level of "More than 100K." If I break down the variables by income groups I get the following results.

Less Than $50K

An LGBT person who has a household income of less than $50K is .776 times less likely to be conservative. A heterosexual person who has a household income of less than $50K is .916 times less likely to be conservative. Finally, the general population shows that a person who has a household income of less than $50K is .885 times less likely to be conservative.

More Than $50K

An LGBT person who has household income of more than $50K is .972 times less likely to be conservative. A heterosexual person who has a household income of more than $50K is .925 times less likely to be conservative. Finally, the general population shows that a person who has a household income of more than $50K is .911 times less likely to be conservative.

More Than $100K

An LGBT person who has household income of more that $100K is .187 times less likely to be conservative. A heterosexual person who has a household income of more than $100K is .849 times less likely to be conservative. Finally, the general population shows that a person who has a household income of more than $100K is .772 times less likely to be conservative.

Again, the LGBT population is different from the heterosexual population. Wealthy LGBTs still identify as liberal whereas higher income heterosexuals would identify as conservative. Out of all the regressions these calculations showed the greatest difference between the LGBT and heterosexual and general population.

Binary Regression of Full-Time Employment

I recoded the full-time employment variables into one group. I recoded "yes" to full-time employment as full-time. In order to create the dummy variables I removed the "no" from my regression. Overall, I found that full-time employment does not have much of an impact on change in ideology for the LGBT population. Also, most of political behavior literature analyzes type of employment, such as blue collar workers are most likely to be liberal (Campbell et al. 1980), not full-time versus part-time employment.

If I break down the variables by religion groups I get the following results.

Full-Time Employment

My full-time LGBT sample or general population calculation is not significant at .491 or .137. However, my heterosexual sample is marginally statistically significant. An LGBT person who is full-time employed is 1.185 times more likely to be conservative. A heterosexual person who is full-time employed is .882 times less likely to be conservative. Finally, the general population suggests a person who is full-time employed is .914 times less likely to be conservative.

In conclusion, it was hypothesized that conservative LGBTs are older, male, white, more highly educated, likely to be partnered or married, largely religious, have higher household income, and more likely to be employed full-time. Overall, my study determined six areas of statistical significance, but mainly for the liberal LGBTs and not the conservative LGBTs. First, the other race variable appears significant, but the odds of being conservative were less likely. Thus, if the other race variable could be determined to be the missing race variable category, such as Latino, it could be determined that liberal LGBT population is not different from the general population in terms of Latinos and liberal voting behavior. Next, graduate school variable looks statistically significant, but the odds of being conservative were less likely. I conclude this is a result from graduate and professional degrees being combined together as a variable. If professional degrees, such as MBAs, were separated, I would have seen a higher conservative response. Third, the nonmarried variable looks statistically significant, but the odds of being conservative were less likely. Thus, the liberal LGBT population is not different from the general population in terms of nonmarried relationships and liberal voting behavior. Next, the partnered variable looks statistically significant, but the odds of being conservative were again less likely. I might posit here that LGBT partnerships are similar to heterosexual partnerships and marriages. I found 33 percent conservative LGBTs were partnered and 37 of the liberal LGBTs were partnered. Thus, this calculation shows the liberal LGBTs are more likely to be partnered (and not married). Although the results did show that the conservative LGBTs were more likely to be married in male-female relationships. Fifth, the none religious variable looks statistically significant, but the odds of being conservative were also less likely. Therefore, nonreligious LGBTs are more likely to be liberal than conservative. Last, the "More than $100K" variable seems statistically significant, but the odds of being conservative were again less likely. This, however, disagrees with the political behavior literature, which suggests the more money a person has, the more likely he or she will be conservative. Hence, the calculation determined that wealthy LGBTs would remain liberal, regardless of income. In other words, LGBTs identify with a sexual identity more than a class identity. So, although the general population identifies as conservative in terms of higher income, this is not the case for LGBTs. Finally, Chapter 6 will review findings, summaries, and conclusions.

Chapter 6

Reinventing Queer: Where Is the LGBT Community Headed?

This work has been concerned with examining conservative LGBTs from the perspective of group identification. The following pages summarize the findings and offers suggestions for further research.

Overall, the study's findings are concerned with two main areas: (1) group identity and group consciousness of conservative LGBTs and (2) demographics of conservative LGBTs. My results indicate that the coming-out experience determines group identity. This process appears to be very different from the establishment of group consciousness for other minority groups who learn that from their childhood they are African American, Latino, and so on. This LGBT group identity then mitigates the effect of other SES factors that would affect political ideology (such as age, income, race, male, straight), which my binary regression tested. On the other hand, these same SES factors should be much stronger for the general population (white, male, straight) who do not experience a group identity effect because they are the dominant group and they may never reflect on how that affects them. So, returning to my central theory, does some other identity trump sexual identity for gay conservatives? My research shows yes, but it appears to be the same factors as those that affect the general population.

With regard to the development of group identity it was hypothesized (hypotheses 1a through 1f) that some LGBTs are conservative despite the fact that the Conservative Party and the manifestation of that ideology in this society are so patently anti-gay; providing little, if any, policies based on sexual identity, which benefit the LGBT

Gay Conservatives: Group Consciousness and Assimilation
© 2007 by The Haworth Press, Inc. All rights reserved.
doi:10.1300/5722_06

community. And do conservative LGBTs disagree with the conservative moniker that is utilized by the neoconservative movement or the religious right? In actuality, do LGBT conservatives politically view themselves as classic libertarians and not as LGBT conservatives?

This major hypothesis and its subparts were supported through email interviews with both leading conservative and liberal LGBTs. Though some of LGBT respondents' answers predictably varied, they did provide a detailed description on conservative LGBTs political attitudes and beliefs. Overall, conservative LGBTs *did not* define themselves in terms of limited government as much as the researcher thought. Nonetheless, conservative LGBTs *did* see a need to receive policies in regards to sexual identity. Conservative LGBTs *did not* see a need to "blend in." On the other hand, conservative LGBTs *did* see LGBT activist demands as "too confrontational." Conservative LGBTs *did not* see LGBTs as an oppressed group. Finally, conservative LGBTs *did not* see an inherent conflict in being LGBT and conservative. - well, duh!

In addition, hypothesis 2 and its subparts (hypotheses 2a through 2h) examined the demographics of conservative LGBTs. They investigated which individual variable levels correlated, such as education and religion, as well as their political identification with conservatives. Could any of these particular demographics explain LGBT political behavior? And how did any one of these factors influence political identification or vote choices? Overall, it was posited that LGBT conservatives appear to focus on economic or other characteristics to determine political choices. In addition, other personal characteristics appear to be influencing conservative LGBTs. The study demonstrated that conservative LGBTs, percentage-wise, appear to be largely (2a) white (92 percent), (2b) male (66 percent), (2c) older (44 percent), (2e) married (36 percent), (2f) belonging to a Christian religion (68 percent), (2g) having higher household incomes (43 percent), and (2h) employed full-time (64 percent). However, I also found liberals were more likely to be (2d) college educated (54 percent) and (2e) partnered (39 percent).

Overall, I found six variable areas, which demonstrated statistical significance in that conservative LGBTs behaved similarly to the general population. Most important, the six variables that were statistically significant were in the same direction as those found to be important in general political ideology literature. Therefore, my research determined that there was statistical significance for conservative LGBTs in relation to the general conservative population. In fact, the data suggests that the overall LGBT population really mirrors the general population in terms of political behavior, except in one area. In terms of high income, liberal LGBTs self-identify more with sexual identity, and remained liberal in terms of policy choices and political behavior. _ not a summary?

In summary, understanding the LGBT community is important for a number of reasons. First, the LGBT community represents a growing and influential political class. Next, minority cohesion is significant in comprehending political behavior. Overall, a group must primarily be cohesive when working with the dominant political group—for example as being the swing voters or key to some group's success. If the group is split, the group's ability will then lessen, with regards to winning any political representation or policy change. Currently, the divide between the conservative LGBTs and liberal LGBTs diminishes the legitimacy of being the all-important swing vote. Thus, as this study concludes, it will describe minority cohesion literature in relation to the LGBT community.

Many political scientists believe that there are many ways to view policy depiction. In fact, some political theorists propose policy delineation is really a set of struggles and tradeoffs between policy representations. For example, some authors suggest policy representation is really a compromise of descriptive representation versus substantive representation. Therefore, they see "descriptive" portrayals as "symbolic"—consequently it's described as a demographic characteristic. Also, they regard "substantive" illustrations as thoughts, in which perception is based on actual "policy."

Lani Guinier (1994) adds another element to the debate. She offers the term of "authentic representation." Guinier states, "Authentic representation describes the psychological value for some people of having similarly situated representation." She feels that through "authentic representation" voters can directly pick a candidate because of shared similar experiences—it is a combination of descriptive and substantive. Specifically, Guinier's electoral research focuses on African Americans. Guinier hypothesizes four underlying assumptions regarding minority electoral strategies, which benefit African Americans through descriptive representation. First, black officials are authentic. Guinier states about authentic representation, "The term is suggestive of the essentialist impulse in black political participation: because black officials are black, they are representative" (p. 20). Thus, I would vote for a GLBT candidate over a straight candidate (assuming equal political qualifications) because the GLBT one understands my shared life experiences. Next, Guinier infers black candidates increase black voter mobilization. She states, "The mobilization assumption measures representation effectiveness based on the ability of black candidates to increase black Election Day turnout" (p. 23). For example, the turnout of LGBT voters is likely to be much more if they have a viable LGBT candidate. Third, the polarization assumption details racial bloc voting. She explains, "The polarization assumption is based on evidence that, absent compelling reasons to do otherwise, whites and blacks vote for persons of their own racial/ ethnic background" (p. 23). Thus, the idea that a majority-straight jurisdiction causes the defeat of an LGBT candidate makes the LGBT candidate pander to the majority-straight to find allies. Last, the responsive assumption targets the less well off. Guinier says, "The responsive assumption suggests that black representatives share the original civil rights vision, which targeted the least well off members of the community" (p. 24). Thus, LGBTs' elected officials are the best hope for the LGBT constituents as these will ultimately benefit from LGBT-centered policies. Also, she suggests minority representation empowerment occurs through a coalition of policy responses based on clientistic leadership, incrementalism, and electoral separateness. However, incrementalism is considered rare; while the other two factors are thought to be more common and essential parts of single member districts (winner take all, majority rule).

Raphael Sonenshein (1993) tells that a de-radicalized strategy works in creating political coalitions between races and might be the most effective in minority electoral strategies. A de-radicalized strategy finds some policy issues that cut across all racial groups. Maybe their primary focus would be on class base issues. For example, conservative LGBTs might have a shared low tax interest with conservative heterosexuals. Also, they might have geographically linked attitudes. Thus, they live in the same regions, and they have the same wants. But in this case do they compete for the same resources? Hence,

Sonenshein (1993) says there are three conditions that significantly determine whether groups will work together in a political coalition: ideology, interest, and leadership trust. First, he states about ideology, "Where liberalism is strongest, both in numbers and in prestige, African Americans' political success ought to be the greatest" (p. 11). Yet, in New York (the center of liberalism) African Americans and liberal whites (mainly Jewish) are not a cohesive group at all. But Guinier would say this is not an "authentic representation" of African Americans. It might be substantive in liberal policy, but it fails to be descriptive. Thus, New York African Americans do not share the same demographic characteristics. Second, Sonenshein details that "interest conflicts grow out of the nature if the city struggles for power and the extent to which the elected city government controls material stakes" (p. 12). This is to say, if African Americans' struggle for power threatens white liberals' power base they will not unite. For example, in New York, African Americans went after the same jobs as the liberal whites. Guinier would suggest this is a substantive representation issue. Last, Sonenshein explains leadership trust is important. However, it would appear that this is significant if they have a shared history. In other words, "Have I worked with these leaders before?" It is most likely that these leaders protect the resources of their own groups first. Therefore, in this instance, Guinier's descriptive representation is occurring. She views minority groups who compete for district representation as diluting the effectiveness of the minority groups. Notwithstanding, in certain instances white liberal swing votes could put African Americans over the top and winning more districts. Thus, she would suggest Africa Americans align with white liberals when possible; although I think she would warn them against aligning with Asians or Latinos. Therefore, LGBTs should position themselves with liberal heterosexuals to create political change, which benefits the LGBT community. However, the increasing numbers of conservative LGBTs lessens the possibility of this alliance.

As society leaps into the twenty-first century the big question is, Where is the LGBT movement headed? Actually, I think a bigger question is, How do LGBT individuals want to be treated by the rest of society? What are they trying to accomplish in the realm of relations with family members, friends, employers, the media and their own LGBT community? That having been said, we are back to the four current schools of thought on this topic.

SEPARATION

The notion of separation comes from the radical queer left point of view of indifference. The best examples are presented in the works of Michael Walker's *Trouble with Normal* and Richard Goldstein's *The Attack Queers*. In other words, one should not care what straight society thinks about LGBTs. Specifically, heterosexual culture or opinion should not corrupt homosexuals' view of self. The Stonewall riots mark the highpoint of this philosophy. Hence, the LGBT society is no longer oppressed by, or dependent on, a community outside of LGBT groups. Thus, gay power frees LGBTs from the chains of shame imposed on by heterosexuals. The greatest thing about this model is the removal of heterosexual disapproval, which often cripples the LGBT community emotionally, intellectually, economically, and politically. Overall, it is popular with many LGBTs, because it creates a microscopic gay "theme park" for the LGBT lifestyle. Unfortunately, heterosexuals make up 90 percent of the real world. So, although this model has had success in areas with higher concentration of LGBT populations, such as urban gay ghettos, it's not always useful in other places. For example, it's not useful to the LGBT youth living in the Midwest whose family or religion has already informed them that their homosexuality is shameful. Also, LGBTs cannot go walking down the street holding hands with their partners in most towns without some type of reaction. It would follow that the LGBT community can act apathetically to heterosexuals, with an "ignorance is bliss" approach, but it is at their own risk.

EMANCIPATION

The idea that the radical gay movement was "disappearing" began in the late 1990s and developed into the short-lived "post gay" movement. The "post gay" movement evolved out of former *Out* magazine editor in chief James Collard's declaration that the LGBT liberation movement was over, and the LGBT community should stop complaining and start spending. Interestingly enough, when the LGBT *Out* magazine's political commentator Michelangelo Signorile left due to Collard's "dumbing down" of the magazine, the movement peaked. Overall, this model believes in an expulsion of sexual identity as a social classification. Thus, individuals are neither classified as LGBT nor straight. In other words, identity based on a person's sexual preference would no longer exist. However, one's sexual identity is similar to an individual's racial or religious identity, in that it is simply not that easy to forget. The model is a nice idea, but sort of a pipe dream. However, it resulted in a reemergence of LGBT left leaders reminding the community we are still oppressed. Now, Bob McCubbin's *The Roots of Lesbian & Gay Oppression: A Marxist View* would suggest that the "post gay movement" meant radical gay liberation lost the battle in the 1990s. But I think 1990s Michelangelo Signorile's *Queer in America* is a strong reminder that the battle has just begun. Until every gay actor, lesbian politician, bisexual gossip columnist, and transgender blue-collar worker can be out without fear or losing one's job, the movement has a long way to go.

MORALIZATION

Overall, Larry Kramer's *Reports from the Holocaust* and his other work have an essential message: "that we must love one another or die" (1994, p. 1). However, recent reports do suggest that HIV infection among young gay men (especially among men of color) is a strong reminder that his forewarning directive is not impacting the gay community like it should. Add to the fact that gay men are using the Internet to cruise for sex such as "bare-backing," like gay men used bathhouses in the 1970s, implies that not much has changed in the sexual behavior of LGBTs. Also, the rise in the use of party drugs, such as ecstasy, GHB, Special K, and crystal meth at gay circuit parties suggests that gay men are not acting as sexually responsible as they should. In addition, Gabriel Rotello's in his *Sexual Ecology* contends that "Larry Kramer's central point, that gay men need to love more and fuck less—is still, like most prophecy, undigested and unaccepted by the very people who need it most" (1997, p. 98). In other words, the prophet Kramer spoke, and we quickly forgot the message. I would be surprised if most of the circuit party aficionados even know who Larry Kramer is, much less Gabriel Rotello.

ASSIMILATION

This fourth school of thought says that the LGBT should seek acceptance from the many heterosexuals around them. This approach developed out of the conservative LGBT movement in the early 1990s. Andrew Sullivan and Bruce Bawer lead the charge that LGBTs should try to act "normal." By doing so, LGBTs would not need special laws for protection because anti-LGBT resentment would not exist. Thus, family, friends, employers, and religions would celebrate and accept the LGBT lifestyle. The problem with this model is that it does not acknowledge that homosexuals are, indeed, different than heterosexuals. Unfortunately, LGBTs are not that accepted by heterosexuals overall. LGBTs still do not have the legal right to get married or openly serve in the military. Many LGBTs believe they still need protective legislation, such as hate crimes. Finally, my research suggests that "assimilationists" are really identifying with either class or race. Is forgetting one's sexual identity in hopes of being accepted by a straight community the answer?

[handwritten margin notes: "Actually' it does?", "Sullivan's book entitled 'virtually normal'", "Not all of them?"]

REINVENTION

Actually, I composed this idea before Madonna used it as the title of her 2004 summer concert. Maybe it is because both of us study Kabbalah teachings. The main point of the religious study is learning to destroy ego and change for the better. Therefore, I label my thought as "reinventing queer." The fact is the LGBT community cannot go forward until the LGBT community is a unified force. The same sex marriage has given the LGBT community a brief romance, but I am afraid it does not look like it will last long.

Moreover, how can this happen with liberal LGBTs attacking the conservative LGBTs as traitors or trying to "assimilate" with heterosexuals? Conversely, conservative LGBTs need to stop calling liberal LGBTs freaks and "un-normal." Heck, what is "normal" anyway? And when I think of post gay, well I just imagine the post that Matthew Shepard's body hung from. Thus, I believe the LGDT community needs to put away its differences and investigate a new path. Honestly, a more centrist LGBT approach is the answer. The LGBT community cannot just ignore heterosexuals. As the saying goes, "Some of my best friends are straight." I do believe that some straights oppress members of the LGBT community; however, I also think LGBTs oppress one another. I do not want to beg to sit at the table of heterosexuals just because there are more of them. Therefore, I would prefer more tolerance and less judgment from heterosexuals.

So, where is the LGBT movement going? I am not sure yet. But I hope this study provided more insight into the LGBT political identity. In the past, an absence of any LGBT identity bruised the community. Presently, it is the split of the LGBT identity that might ultimately harm the community. Thus, for the future I'm optimistic that as a community one can find a common ground of understanding between both political groups. This study was a small attempt to do just that.

[handwritten margin note:] Classic!

[handwritten note at bottom:] Complete missed opportunity with the rich data he had → missed nuances in favour of a rigid hierarchy → Does identity really work in such a manner?

Appendix

Characteristics of the Sample

TABLE A.1

Age characteristics	18-34	35-44	45-54	55+	Total
Gender					
Male	16	21	21	20	78
Female	15	14	7	4	40
Education					
Some high school	2	0	1	1	4
High school graduate	3	5	4	4	16
Some college	16	17	5	9	47
College graduate	8	9	12	3	32
Some graduate school	0	3	3	5	11
Graduate school graduate	2	1	3	2	8
Household Income					
Less than $15,000	3	0	2	1	6
$15,000 to $24,999	4	3	4	3	14
$25,000 to $34,999	5	4	2	1	12
$35,000 to $49,999	3	9	3	7	22
$50,000 to $74,999	6	12	9	6	33
$75,000 to $99,999	4	3	4	2	13
$100,000 to $124,999	0	3	0	1	4
$125,000 to $149,999	0	0	1	0	1
Decline to answer	6	1	3	3	13
Marital status					
Married	9	12	10	11	42
Nonmarried	10	8	11	8	37
Living with a partner	12	15	7	5	39

Gay Conservatives: Group Consciousness and Assimilation
© 2007 by The Haworth Press, Inc. All rights reserved.
doi:10.1300/5722_07

TABLE A .1 *(continued)*

Age characteristics	18-34	35-44	45-54	55+	Total
Religious preferences					
Catholic	2	7	8	4	21
Christian	9	15	6	5	35
Greek Orthodox	1	0	0	0	1
Protestant	4	4	5	8	21
Other	7	10	2	3	21
None	6	1	4	3	14
Decline to answer	2	1	1	1	5
Race					
White	26	34	27	22	109
Black	1	0	0	1	2
Asian	1	0	0	0	1
Other	2	0	0	1	3
Decline to answer	1	1	0	1	3

TABLE A.2

Gender characteristics	Male	Female	Total
Age			
18-34	16	15	31
35-44	21	14	35
45-54	21	7	28
55+	20	4	24
Education			
Some high school	0	4	4
High school graduate	8	8	16
Some college	28	19	47
College graduate	25	7	32
Some graduate school	11	0	11
Graduate school graduate	6	2	8
Household income			
Less than $15,000	3	3	6
$15,000 to $24,999	9	5	14

TABLE A.2 *(continued)*

Gender characteristics	Male	Female	Total
$25,000 to $34,999	10	2	12
$35,000 to $49,999	17	5	22
$50,000 to $74,999	18	15	33
$75,000 to $99,999	10	3	13
$100,000 to $124,999	4	0	4
$125,000 to $149,999	1	0	1
Decline to answer	6	7	13
Marital status			
Married	26	16	42
Nonmarried	26	11	37
Living with a partner	26	13	39
Religious preferences			
Catholic	14	7	21
Christian	21	14	35
Greek Orthodox	0	1	1
Protestant	15	6	21
Other	14	7	21
None	12	2	14
Decline to answer	2	3	5
Race			
White	73	36	109
Black	1	1	2
Asian	0	1	1
Other	1	2	3
Decline to answer	3	0	3

TABLE A.3

Race characteristics	White	African American	Asian	Other	Decline	Total
Gender						
Male	73	1	0	1	3	78
Female	36	1	1	0	2	40

TABLE A.3 *(continued)*

Race characteristics	White	African American	Asian	Other	Decline	Total
Age						
18-34	26	1	1	2	1	31
35-44	34	0	0	0	1	35
45-54	27	0	0	0	0	27
55+	22	1	0	1	1	25
Education						
Some high school	3	0	0	1	0	4
High school graduate	13	2	0	0	1	16
Some college	43	0	1	1	2	47
College graduate	31	0	0	1	0	32
Some graduate school	11	0	0	0	0	11
Graduate school graduate	8	0	0	0	0	8
Household income						
Less than $15,000	5	0	0	1	0	6
$15,000 to $24,999	13	1	0	0	0	14
$25,000 to $34,999	11	0	0	0	1	12
$35,000 to $49,999	20	1	0	0	1	22
$50,000 to $74,999	31	0	1	1	0	33
$75,000 to $99,999	12	0	0	0	1	13
$100,000 to $124,999	4	0	0	0	0	4
$125,000 to $149,999	1	0	0	0	0	1
Decline to answer	12	0	0	1	0	13
Marital status						
Married	36	2	1	2	1	42
Nonmarried	35	0	0	1	1	37
Living with a partner	38	0	0	0	1	39
Religious preferences						
Catholic	21	0	0	0	0	21
Christian	31	1	0	1	2	35
Greek Orthodox	1	0	0	0	0	1
Protestant	21	0	0	0	0	21
Other	17	1	1	1	1	21
None	13	0	0	1	0	14
Decline to answer	5	0	0	0	0	5

TABLE A.4

Education characteristics	Some HS	HS Grad.	Some College	College Grad.	Some Grad. School	Grad. School Grad.	Total
Gender							
Male	0	8	28	25	11	6	78
Female	4	8	19	7	0	2	40
Age							
18-34	2	3	16	8	0	2	31
35-44	0	5	17	9	3	1	35
45-54	1	4	5	12	3	3	27
55+	1	4	9	3	5	2	25
Household income							
Less than $15,000	0	1	1	2	1	1	6
$15,000 to $24,999	1	3	8	2	0	0	14
$25,000 to $34,999	0	1	6	5	0	0	12
$35,000 to $49,999	0	3	8	8	3	0	22
$50,000 to $74,999	1	4	12	10	4	2	33
$75,000 to $99,999	0	2	4	2	2	3	13
$100,000 to $124,999	0	0	3	0	1	0	4
$125,000 to $149,999	0	0	0	0	0	1	1
Decline to answer	2	2	5	3	0	1	13
Race							
White	3	13	43	31	11	8	109
Black	0	2	0	0	0	0	2
Asian	0	0	1	0	0	0	1
Other	1	0	1	1	0	0	3
Decline to answer	0	1	2	0	0	0	3
Marital status							
Married	2	9	17	8	4	2	42
Nonmarried	1	2	12	14	4	4	37
Living with a partner	1	5	18	10	3	2	39
Religious preferences							
Catholic	2	2	9	6	1	1	21
Christian	1	5	14	9	2	4	35
Greek Orthodox	0	1	0	0	0	0	1
Protestant	0	3	5	8	4	1	21

TABLE A.4 *(continued)*

Education characteristics	Some HS	HS Grad.	Some College	College Grad.	Some Grad. School	Grad. School Grad.	Total
Other	0	3	8	7	1	2	21
None	0	2	8	2	2	0	14
Decline to answer	1	0	3	0	1	0	5

TABLE A.5

Marital characteristics	Married	Nonmarried	Partnered	Total
Gender				
Male	26	26	26	78
Female	16	11	13	40
Age				
18-34	9	10	12	31
35-44	12	8	15	35
45-54	10	11	7	28
55+	11	8	5	24
Education				
Some high school	2	1	1	4
High school graduate	9	2	5	16
Some college	17	12	18	47
College graduate	8	14	10	32
Some graduate school	4	4	3	11
Graduate school graduate	2	4	2	8
Household income				
Less than $15,000	1	4	1	6
$15,000 to $24,999	5	6	3	14
$25,000 to $34,999	2	6	4	12
$35,000 to $49,999	7	5	10	22
$50,000 to $74,999	16	6	11	33
$75,000 to $99,999	4	4	5	13
$100,000 to $124,999	2	1	1	4
$125,000 to $149,999	0	1	0	1
Decline to answer	5	4	4	13

TABLE A.5 *(continued)*

Marital characteristics	Married	Nonmarried	Partnered	Total
Religious preferences				
Catholic	8	5	8	21
Christian	11	13	11	35
Greek Orthodox	0	0	1	1
Protestant	10	7	4	21
Other	8	7	6	21
None	4	5	5	14
Decline to answer	1	0	4	5
Race				
White	36	35	38	109
Black	2	0	0	2
Asian	1	0	0	1
Other	2	1	0	3
Decline to answer	1	1	1	3

TABLE A.6

Religion characteristics	Cath.	Chris.	Greek Ortho.	Prot.	Other	None	Decline to answer	Total
Gender								
Male	14	21	0	15	14	12	2	78
Female	7	14	1	6	7	2	3	40
Age								
18-34	2	9	1	4	7	6	2	31
35-44	7	15	0	4	10	1	1	35
45-54	8	6	0	5	2	4	1	27
55+	4	5	0	8	3	3	1	25
Household income								
Less than $15,000	0	1	0	2	2	1	0	6
$15,000 to $24,999	1	7	0	0	2	3	1	14
$25,000 to $34,999	1	3	0	2	3	2	1	12
$35,000 to $49,999	4	4	0	4	4	4	2	22
$50,000 to $74,999	7	11	0	9	5	1	0	33
$75,000 to $99,999	3	5	1	1	2	1	0	13
$100,000 to $124,999	1	0	0	1	1	1	0	4

TABLE A.6 *(continued)*

Religion characteristics	Cath.	Chris.	Greek Ortho.	Prot.	Other	None	Decline to answer	Total
$125,000 to $149,999	0	1	0	0	0	0	0	1
Decline to answer	4	3	0	2	2	1	1	13
Education								
Some high school	2	1	0	0	0	0	1	4
High school graduate	2	5	1	3	3	2	0	16
Some college	9	14	0	5	8	8	3	47
College graduate	6	9	0	8	7	2	0	32
Some graduate school	1	2	0	4	1	2	1	11
Graduate school graduate	1	4	0	1	2	0	0	8
Marital status								
Married	8	11	0	10	8	4	1	42
Nonmarried	5	13	0	7	7	5	0	37
Living with a partner	8	11	1	4	6	5	4	39
Race								
White	21	31	1	21	17	13	5	109
Black	0	1	0	0	1	0	0	2
Asian	0	0	0	0	1	0	0	1
Other	0	1	0	0	1	1	0	3
Decline to answer	0	2	0	0	1	0	0	3

References

Chapter 1

Baumgartner FD, Jones BD. *Agendas and Instability in American Politics.* Chicago, University of Chicago Press, 1993.

Bentley AF. *The Process of Government: A Study of Social Pressures.* Chicago, University of Chicago Press, 1908.

Colapinto J. The Young Hipublicans. *New York Times Magazine.* May 25, 2003: 1. http://www.nytimes.com/2003/05/25/magazine/25 REPUBLICANS.html, May 25, 2003.

Conover PJ. The influence of group identification on political perception and evaluation. *Journal of Politics* 1984; 46: 760-785.

D'Emilio J. *Sexual Politics, Sexual Communities.* Chicago, University of Chicago Press, 1983.

Gates G. *Gay and Lesbian Families in the United States: Same-Sex Unmarried Partner Households.* Washington, DC, The Urban Institute, 2001.

Gill Foundation. *Out of the Closet and into the Voting Booth: Lesbian, Gay, Bisexual and Transgender Voters in 2000.* Denver, CO, Gill Foundation, 2001.

Goldstein R. *The Attack Queers.* London, Verso, 2002.

Goodridge v. Dept. of Public Health, 798 N.E.2d 941 (Massachusetts 2003).

Hertzog M. *The Lavender Vote: Gays, Lesbians and Bisexuals in American Electoral Politics.* New York, New York University Press, 1996.

Jacques C. *Answers to Questions About Marriage Equality.* Washington, DC, Human Rights Campaign, 2003.

Kaiser, HJ, Kaiser Family Foundation. *Lesbian, Gay and Bisexual Survey: Inside-Out: A Report on the Experiences of Lesbians, Gays and Bisexuals in America and the Public's View on Issues and Polices Related to Sexual Orientation.* San Francisco, California, Kaiser Family Foundation, November 2001.

Kinder D, Winter N. Exploring the racial divide: Blacks, Whites, and opinion on national policy. *American Journal of Political Science* 2001; 45: 439-456.

Kinsey AC, Pomeroy WB, Martin CE. *Sexual Behavior in the Human Male.* Philadelphia, W.B. Saunders and Company, 1948.

Kirchick J. Off the fence: Anti-jag policy quashes law students' free speech rights. *Yale Daily News,* October 15, 2003: 2.

Kurtz S. Beyond gay marriage. *The Weekly Standard,* August 4, 2002; 8(45): 1-12.

Laumann E, Gagnon J, Michael R, Michaels S. *The Social Organization of Sexuality*. Chicago, University of Chicago Press, 1994.

Miller AH, Gurin P, Gurin G, Malanchuk O. Group consciousness and political participation. *American Journal of Political Science* 1981; 25(3): 494-511.

Osburn DC. New gay discharge figures up 73% since Don't Ask, don't tell. Service Members Legal Defense Network, 2000, www.sldn.org.

Rotello G. *Sexual Ecology: AIDS and the Destiny of Man*. New York, Dutton Adult, 1997.

Sullivan A. If it's not a crime to be gay, why can't we get married? *The Wall Street Journal*. October 8, 2003.

———. *Love Undetectable*. New York, Vintage, 1999a.

———. TRB: After life 1999b; *The New Republic* 221(21): 6.

———. Here comes the groom: A (conservative) case for gay marriage. *The New Republic* 1989; 201(9): 20, 22.

Truman D. *The Governmental Process*. New York, Alfred Knopf, 1951.

Varnell P. DADT unravels further. *The Chicago Free Press,* November 22, 2002: 2.

Yang A. *From Wrong to Right*. Washington, DC, The Policy Institute of National Gay Lesbian Task Force, 1999, p. 12.

Chapter 2

Armesto JC, Weisman AG. Attributions and emotional reactions to the identity disclosure ("coming out") of a homosexual child. *Family Process* 2001; 40(2): 145-161.

Axelrod R. *Evolution of Cooperation.* New York, Basic Books, 1984.

Beaty L. Identity development of homosexual youth and parental and familial influences on the coming out process. *Adolescence* 1999; 34: 597.

Bentley AF. *The Process of Government: A Study of Social Pressures*. Chicago, University of Chicago Press, 1908.

Berelson BR, Lazarsfeld PF, McPhee WN. *Voting: A Study of Opinion Formation in a Presidential Campaign*. Chicago, University of Chicago Press, 1954.

Bobo L, Zubrinsky CL, Johnson JH, Jr., Oliver ML. Public opinion before and after a spring of discontent. In Mark B (ed.): *The 1992 Los Angeles Riots: Lessons for the Urban Future*. Boulder, CO, Westview Press, 1994.

Browning R, Marshall DR, Tabb D. *Racial Politics in American Cities*. New York, Longman, 2003.

Browning R, Marshall DR, Tabb, D. *Racial Politics in American Cities: Blacks and Hispanics in the US—Political Mobilization, Power and Prospects*. New York, Taylor and Frances Books Ltd., 1990.

Cain BE, Kiewiet DR, Uhlaner CJ. The acquisition of partisanship by Latinos and Asian Americans. *American Journal of Political Science* 1991; 35: 390-422.

Cain BE, Kiewiet DR, Uhlaner CJ. Political participation of ethnic minorities in the 1980s. *Political Behavior,* September 11, 1989, 195-231.

Calhoun JC. *A Disquisition on Government: And Selections from the Discourse.* New York, Hackett Publishing Company, 1853; Reprint edition (October 1, 1993).

Campbell A, Converse PE, Miller WE, Stokes DE. *The American Voter.* Chicago, University of Chicago Press, 1960; Reprint edition (September 1980).

Cass V. Homosexual identity formation: Testing a theoretical model. *The Journal of Research* 1984; 20(2): 143-167.

Chong D. *Collective Action and the Civil Rights Movement.* Chicago, University of Chicago Press, 1991.

Cross WE. The Negro to black conversion experience: Towards the psychology of black liberation. *Black World* 1971; 20: 13-27.

Dahl R. *Who Governs?* New Haven, CT, Yale University Press, 1961, p. 10.

Dahl R. *A Preface to Democratic Theory,* Chicago, University of Chicago Press, 1956, p. 30.

D'Augelli AR, Hershberger SL, Pilkington NW. Lesbian, gay, and bisexual youths and their families: Disclosure of sexual orientation and its consequences. *American Journal of Orthopsychiatry* 1998; 68: 361-371.

De Tocqueville A. *Democracy in America.* New York, Signet Book, 1835; Reprint edition (September 1, 2001).

Downing NE, Roush KL. From passive acceptance to active commitment: A model of feminist identity development for women. *The Counseling Psychologist* 1985; 13(4): 695-709.

Dubé EM, Savin-Williams RC. Sexual identity development among ethnic sexual-minority male youths. *Developmental Psychology* 1999; 35: 1389-1399.

Etheridge M. Collective action, public policy and class conflict. *Western Political Quarterly* 1987; 40: 575-592.

Gamson W. *Power and Discontent.* Homewood, Illinois, The Dorsey Press, 1968.

Gartner ST, Segura G. Appearances can be deceptive. *Rationality and Society* 1997; 9: 131-161.

Graves S, Lee J. Ethnic underpinnings of voting preferences: Latinos and the 1996 U.S. senate election in Texas. *Social Science Quarterly* 2000; 81: 226-236.

Hamilton A, Jay J, Madison J. *The Federalist Papers.* New York, Signet Classics, 2003 (Reprint edition).

Hansen J. Political economy of group membership. *American Political Science Review* 1985; 79: 79-96; New York, Signet Classics Reprint edition (April 1, 2003).

Hertzog M. *The Lavender Vote: Gays, Lesbians and Bisexuals in American Electoral Politics.* New York, New York University Press, 1996.

Jones-Correa M, Leal DL. Becoming "Hispanic": Secondary panethnic identification among Latin American-origin populations in the United States. *Hispanic Journal of Behavioral Sciences* 1996; 18: 214-254.

Knowes A, Neeley G. Toward an explanation for public interest group formation and proliferation: "Seed money, disturbances, entrepreneurship and patronage," *Policy Studies Journal* 1996; 24: 74-88.

Laski H. *Authority in the Modern State.* New Haven, CT, Yale University Press, 1919, p. 346.

Lien P, Collet C, Wong J, Ramakrishnan SK. Asian Pacific American public opinion and political participation. *PS: Political Science & Politics* 2001; 34: 625-631.

Miller AH, Gurin P, Gurin G, Malanchuk O. Group consciousness and political participation. *American Journal of Political Science* 1981; 5(3): 494-511.

Moe T. Toward a broader view of interest groups. *Journal of Politics* 1981; 43: 531-543.

Olsen ME. The social and political participation of blacks. *American Sociological Review* 1970; 35(4): 682-696.

Olson M. *The Logic of Collective Action.* Cambridge, MA, Harvard University Press, 1965.

Orum A. A reappraisal of the social and political participation of Negroes. *American Journal of Sociology* 1966; 72: 32-46.

Sabatier PA. Interest group membership and organization: Multiple theories. In Petracca MB (ed.): *The Politics of Interests: Interest Groups Transformed.* Boulder, CO, Westview Press, 1992, pp. 99-129.

Sabatier PA, McLaughlin SM. Belief congruence between interest-group leaders and members: An empirical analysis of three theories and a suggested synthesis. *Journal of Politics* 1990; 52: 914-935.

Schattschenider EE. *Politics, Pressures and the Tariff.* New York, Prentice Hall, 1935.

Shaw D, de la Garza RO, Lee J. Examining Latino turnout in 1996: A three-state, validated survey approach. *American Journal of Political Science* April 2000; 44(2): 332-340.

Shingles R. Black consciousness and political participation: The missing link. *The American Political Science Review* 1981; 75(1): 76-91.

Sullivan G. A bibliographic guide to government hearings and reports, legislative action, and speeches made in the house. *Journal of Homosexuality* 1984; 10(1-2): 135-189.

Tate K. *From Protest to Politics.* Cambridge, MA, Harvard University Press, 1994.

Troiden RR. The formation of homosexual identities. In Herdt G. (ed.): *Gay and Lesbian Youth.* Binghamton, NY, Harrington Park Press, 1989, pp. 43-73.

Truman D. *The Governmental Process.* New York, Alfred Knopf, 1951, p. 56.

Verba S, Nie NH. *Participation in America.* New York, Harper and Row, 1972.

Walker J. *Mobilizing Interest Groups in America.* Michigan, University of Michigan Press, 1991.

Chapter 3

Adams B. *The Rise of Gay and Lesbian Movement.* New York, Twayne Publishers, 1995.

Bawer B. *A Place at the Table.* New York, Simon and Schuster, 1993.

Crossen, C. Shock troops: AIDS activist group harasses and provokes to make its point, *Wall Street Journal,* December 7, 1989; A1, A9.

D'Emilio J. *Sexual Politics Sexual Communities.* Chicago, Chicago University Press, 1983.

Gartner SS, Seguara GM. Appearances can be deceiving: Self-selection, social group identification, and political mobilization. *Rationality and Society* 1997; 9(2): 133-161.

Hertzog M. *The Lavender Vote.* New York, New York University Press, 1996.

Kramer L. *Reports from the Holocaust.* New York, St. Martin's Press, 1994.

Lee Badgett AMV, Rogers MA. "Left out of the count: Missing same-sex couples in Census 2000," Amherst, MA, Institute for Gay and Lesbian Strategic Studies, 2003.

Marotta T. *The Politics of Homosexuality.* Boston, Houghton Mifflin Company, 1981.

Miller AH, Gurin P, Gurin G, Malanchuk O. Group consciousness and political participation. *American Journal of Political Science* 1981; 25(10): 494-511.

Shilts R. *And the Band Played On: Politics, People, and the AIDS Epidemic.* New York: St. Martin's Press, 1987.

Signorile M. *Queer in America.* New York, Random House, 1993.

Sullivan A. *Virtually Normal.* New York, Random House, 1996.

Washington BT. *Up from Slavery.* New York, Signet Classics, 1901; Reprint edition (January 1, 2000).

Chapter 4

Armesto JC. Attributions and emotional reactions to the identity disclosure of a homosexual child—"Coming out." *Family Process* 2001; 40: 145-161.

Campbell A, Converse PE, Miller WE. Stokes DE. *The American Voter* (Unabridged). New York, Wiley, 1960.

Dubé, EM, Savin-Williams RC. Sexual identity development among ethnic sexual-minority male youths. *Developmental Psychology* 1999; 35: 1389-1399.

Haider-Markel D, Joslyn M, Kniss CJ. Minority group interests and political representation: Gay elected officials in the policy process. *The Journal of Politics* 2000; 62(2): 568-577.

Jennings KM. *Continuities in Political Action: A Longitudinal Study of Political Orientations in Three Western Democracies.* New York, Walter De Gruyte, Inc., 1990.

Lewis GB, Rogers MA, Kenneth S. Sexual identity, sexual behavior, and group socialization: Does gay sex turn people into liberal democrats? Presented at the 2003 Annual Meeting of the American Association for Public Opinion Research, 2003.

Miller WE, Shanks JM. *The New American Voter.* Cambridge, MA, Harvard University Press, 1996.

Ritch S-W, Berndt T. Friendship and peer relations. In Feldman SS, Elliott, GR (eds): *At the Threshold: The Developing Adolescent.* Cambridge, MA, Harvard University Press, 1990, pp. 277-307.

Shernoff M. Family therapy for lesbian and gay clients. *Social Work,* 1984; 29(4): 393-396.

Sherrill K. 2003. Sexual orientation, sexual behavior, and political behavior. Chicago, AAPOR, Sherill.

Tate K. *From Protest to Politics: The New Black Voters in American Elections,* Enlarged Edition. Cambridge, MA, Harvard University Press and the Russell Sage Foundation, 1994.

Chapter 5

Cain BE, Kiewiet DR, Uhlaner CJ. The acquisition of partisanship by Latinos and Asian Americans. *American Journal of Political Science* 1991; 35: 390-422.

Campbell A, Converse PE, Miller WE, Stokes, DE. *The American Voter.* Chicago, University of Chicago Press, 1980.

Dawson M. *Behind the Mule: Race and Class in African American Politics.* Princeton, NJ, Princeton University Press, 1994.

Gill Foundation. *Out of the Closet and Into the Voting Booth: Lesbian, Gay, Bisexual and Transgender Voters in 2000.* Denver, CO: Gill Foundation, 2001.

Kaufmann K, Petrocik J. The changing politics of American men: Understanding the sources of the gender gap. *American Journal of Political Science* July 1999; 43.

Manza J, Brooks C. The religious factor in U.S. presidential elections, 1960 to 1992. *American Journal of Sociology* July 1997;103: 38-81.

Warren C. *Identity and Community in the Gay World.* New York, John Wiley and Sons, 1974.

Weisberg HF. The demographics of a new voting gap: Marital differences in American voting. *Public Opinion Quarterly* 1987; 51: 335-343.

Chapter 6

Goldstein R. *The Attack Queers.* London, Verso, 2002.

Guinier L. *The Tyranny of the Majority.* New York, Free Press, 1994.

Kramer L. *Reports from the Holocaust: The Story of an Aids Activist.* New York, St. Martin's Press, 1994.

McCubbin B. *The Roots of Lesbian & Gay Oppression: A Marxist View.* New York: WW Publishers, 1976.

Rotello G. *Sexual Ecology: AIDS and the Destiny of Man.* New York, Dutton Adult, 1997.

Signorile M. *Queer in America: Sex, the Media, and the Closets of Power.* New York, Random House, 1993.

Sonenshein R. *Politics in Black and White.* New Jersey, Princeton University Press, 1993.

Index

Page numbers followed by the letter "f" indicate figures; those followed by the letter "t" indicate tables.

Gay Conservatives: Group Consciousness and Assimilation
© 2007 by The Haworth Press, Inc. All rights reserved.
doi:10.1300/5722_09

Printed in Great Britain
by Amazon